I0764393

IN THE SHADOW OF DEATH

GENERAL P. H. KRITZINGER

AND MR. R. D. MCDONALD

In the Shadow of Death

P. H. Kritzinger and R. D. McDonald

PO Box 2211
Fairfield, IA 52556
www.1stworldlibrary.com
First Edition

LCCN: 2007930824

Softcover ISBN: 978-1-4218-4856-3
Hardcover ISBN: 978-1-4218-4759-7
eBook ISBN: 978-1-4218-4953-9

1st World Library Literary Society

Giving Back to the World

"If you want to work on the core problem, it's early school literacy."

- James Barksdale, former CEO of Netscape

"No skill is more crucial to the future of a child, or to a democratic and prosperous society, than literacy."

- Los Angeles Times

"Literacy... means far more than learning how to read and write... The aim is to transmit... knowledge and promote social participation."

- UNESCO

"Literacy is not a luxury, it is a right and a responsibility. If our world is to meet the challenges of the twenty-first century we must harness the energy and creativity of all our citizens."

- President Bill Clinton

"Parents should be encouraged to read to their children, and teachers should be equipped with all available techniques for teaching literacy, so the varying needs and capacities of individual kids can be taken into account."

- Hugh Mackay

PREFACE

Several excellent works have already been written about the Anglo-Boer War of the beginning of the twentieth century; but the field of operations was so extensive, the duration of the war so long, and the leaders, on the Boer side, were necessarily so independent of one another in the operations that were conducted with one common aim, that something of interest may well remain to be said. We have not here chronicled our experiences and adventures in the form of a diary, but have rather grouped together events and observations. We write as Boers, frankly regretting the loss of that independence for which we took the field; but also as those who wish to give no offence to any honourable opponent. Our aim has been to do equal justice to both sides in the war; to unite and reconcile, not to separate and embitter, two Christian peoples destined to live together in one land.

"In the Shadow of Death" is a title the reader will hardly consider inappropriate by the time he reaches the end of this little book. Outnumbered on the battlefield, often exposed to the enemy's fire, and one of us wounded and laid low on a bed of intense suffering, and then charged before a Military Court with the greatest of crimes, we did not dare to hope that we should live to write these pages.

And here let our cordial thanks be given to Advocate F.G. Gardiner for his inestimable services in the hour of need, and for kindly submitting to us the "papers" bearing on the trial.

P.H. KRITZINGER.

R.D. MCDONALD.

CONTENTS

CHAPTER I

ANTECEDENTS

> The child is father to the man;
> And I could wish my days to be
> Bound each to each by natural piety.
>
> —*Wordsworth*

A few preliminary pages of personal history I offer to those who followed me either in thought or deed during the Anglo-Boer War.

My ancestors were Germans; my grandfather was born in the South. About the year 1820 he, along with two brothers, bade farewell to the land of his nativity and emigrated to South Africa. They found a home for themselves in the neighbourhood of Port Elizabeth, and there they settled as farmers. Two of the brothers married women of Dutch extraction; one died a bachelor. A small village, Humansdorp, situated near to Port Elizabeth, was the birth-place of my father. There he spent the greater part of his life. He, too, married a Dutch lady; and we children adopted the language of our mother, and spoke Dutch rather than German.

My father took an active part in several of the early Kaffir Wars, and rendered assistance to the Colonial forces in subjugating the native tribes in the Eastern Province of the Cape Colony. With rapt attention and enthusiasm we children would listen to him as he told the tale of those early native wars. I then thought that there was nothing so sublime and glorious as war. My imagination was inflamed, and I longed intensely to participate in such exciting adventures. My experience of recent years has corrected my views. I think differently now. Peace is better than war. War is brutal and damnable. It is indeed "hell let loose."

On the 20th of April, 1870, the arrival of a little Kritzinger was announced on the farm Wildeman's-Kraal, Port Elizabeth District. That little fellow happened to be myself. I do not recollect much of the days of my youth—save that I was of a very lively disposition, with a fondness for all sorts of fun, and often of mischief, which landed me occasionally in great trouble. My parents obeyed the injunctions of Holy Writ in diligently applying the rod when they thought it necessary. As a child, I could but dimly understand, and scarcely believe, that love was at the root of every chastisement.

At the age of five I met with a serious accident. While gathering shells on the beach at Port Elizabeth, the receding waves drew me seaward with irresistible power. But for the pluck and courage of my little playfellow, a lassie of some twelve summers, I was lost. She came to the rescue. I was saved at the last moment: a few seconds more and I must have perished in the deep.

In 1882 my parents, leaving Cape Colony in search of a new home in the Orange Free State, settled down in the district of Ladybrand. It was, however, decided that I should remain behind with an uncle. This uncle was my godfather, and had promised to provide for my education. Having no children, he made me his adopted son. However excellent these arrangements might be, I resolved that I too should go to the Orange Free State. I succeeded in persuading my brother, who had charge of the waggons, to let me follow him on horseback under cover of darkness. I left my uncle's home alone and at dusk on the third evening after my brother's departure. How I felt, and in what condition I was, after riding thirty-five miles on the bare back of a horse, I shall not describe. My parents, who had gone ahead of the waggons, were not a little astonished, and yet they were not angry, at the unexpected appearance of the boy that was left behind.

On my arrival in the Free State it so happened that there was then a dispute as to headship between two Barolong chiefs. This quarrel called forth the intervention of the Free State Government. The burghers were commandoed in the event of resistance on the part of the native chiefs; and I, though a mere boy, at once offered my services to the nearest Field Cornet. He declined to accept them on the score that I was too young. Like David, I was loth to go back home. I borrowed an old gun, got a horse, and off I stole to the Boer commando. The dispute was amicably settled. Some thirty Barolongs, however, offered resistance. Most eagerly I thus fired my first shot upon a human being. I did not know then that it would not be the last; that I should live to hear the mountains and hills of South Africa reverberate with the sound of exploding shells, that the whizz of bullets would assail my ears like the humming of bees; that a bullet would penetrate my own lungs, leaving me a mass of bleeding clay on the battle-field. I did not know that South Africa's plains would yet be drenched with the blood of Boer and Briton until the very rivers ran crimson.

At the early age of seventeen I left the parental roof to earn for myself an independent living. I went to the district of Rouxville, where I occupied a farm situated on the Basutoland border. Several of the Basuto chiefs I got to know well. They allowed me to purchase all I desired from their subjects. Occupied thus with my private affairs while years sped by, I unconsciously drifted on to the disastrous war.

My mind was never absorbed nor disturbed by the many political controversies and problems of South Africa, not that I was indifferent to the welfare of my people and country, for, once war was declared by the leaders, my services were ready. I attached myself to the Rouxville Commando, under Commandant J. Olivier, as a private burgher. When Prinsloo surrendered, late in 1900, I was appointed Assistant-Commandant over that portion of the Rouxville Commando which had refused to lay down arms on Prinsloo's authority. This was my first commission in the Boer Army. On more than one occasion I had been requested to accept appointments; but, realising the great responsibility involved in leadership, I preferred to fight as a private. But events pushed onward; and on the 26th of August, 1900, when Commandant Olivier made an unsuccessful attack on Winburg, which resulted in his capture, I was elected in his stead, and so became Commandant of the Rouxville Commando.

On December 16th, 1900, carrying out instructions of General De Wet, I crossed the Orange River at a point near Odendaal's Stroom, with about 270 burghers. General De Wet was to follow me, but he was prevented. The enemy, determined to drive me back or effect my capture, concentrated numerous forces on my small commando. For months I was dreadfully harassed, and had no rest day or night. But I was resolved neither to retrace my steps nor to capitulate. How I escaped from time to time I now tell. The Cape Colonist Boers began to come in, and my forces increased rather than decreased. The burghers I had at my disposal I subdivided into smaller commandos, to give employment to the enemy, so that they could not concentrate all their forces on me. Thus, as the Colonists rose in arms, the commandos began to multiply more and more, until it was impossible for the British forces to expel the invaders from the Cape Colony.

At the beginning of August, 1901, General French once more fixed his attention on me. I was hard pressed by large forces, and had to fall back on the Orange Free State, where I then operated till the 15th of December. Again, and now for the last time, I forded the Orange River at midnight, and set foot on British territory. The following day I was wounded while crossing the railway line near Hanover Road. For about a month I was laid up in the British hospital at Naauwpoort, whence I was removed to Graaf Reinet gaol, and there I was confined as a criminal until the 10th of March, 1902, when after a five days' trial for murder I was acquitted. After my acquittal I was advanced to the honour (?) of P.O.W. (Prisoner of War), and so remained till the cessation of hostilities.

CHAPTER II

DARK DAYS

> Oft expectation fails, and most oft there where most it promises.
>
> —*Shakespeare*

Up to the 27th February, 1900, the Republican arms were on the whole successful. The Boers fought well and many a brilliant victory crowned their efforts, and encouraged them to continue their struggle for freedom. True, they had to sacrifice many noble lives, but that was a sacrifice they were prepared to make for their country. Fortune smiled on them; as yet they had met with no very serious reverses. Magersfontein, Stormberg, Colenso, Spion Kop, were so many offerings of scarce vanquished Boers to the veiled Goddess Liberty. But towards the end of February, 1900, clouds gathered over the Republics. The tide of fortune was turned; disaster after disaster courted the Boer forces; blow after blow struck them with bewildering force. Then came the news of Cronje's capture. No sooner had we crossed the Orange River during the retreat from Stormberg than we learnt that stunning news of the disaster at Paardeberg on the 27th of February—the anniversary of Amajuba. Cronje captured—the General in whom we had placed such implicit confidence and on whom we relied for the future! Cronje captured—the man who had successfully checked the advance of the English forces on Kimberley at Magersfontein; the hero of many a battle; the man who knew no fear! His men captured—the flower and pick of the Boer forces, with all their guns, and brave Major Albrecht as well!

Many a burgher who up to that fatal day had fought hopefully and courageously lost hope and courage then. Some, we regret to say, were so disconsolate that they renounced their faith in that Supreme Being in whose hands are the destinies of nations. Their reliance on their country's God ended with Cronje's capture, as though their deliverance depended solely upon him. This, however, does not appear so strange when one recollects that the Boers could not afford to lose so many of their best men at a time when all were precious for their country's safety. As to the siege itself, we, not having been in it, cannot enter into its details. One of the besieged, who, in spite of a terrific bombardment and repeated attacks by the enemy, kept a diary of the events of each day, gives this striking description on the 10th and last day:

> "Bombardment heavier than usual. The burghers are recalcitrant and in consequence the General's authority wanes rapidly. There is hardly any food, the remaining bags of biscuits are yellow from the lyddite fumes, so is everything, damp and yellow. The stench of the decomposed horses and oxen is awful. The water of the rivers is putrid with carrion. A party of men caught three stray sheep early on the morning of the 10th. In haste they killed them and started to skin them desperately; but they had half done when a lyddite shell bursting close to them turned the mutton yellow with its fumes and it had to be abandoned reluctantly. The sufferings of the wounded are heartrending. Little children huddled together in bomb-proof

excavations are restless, hungry and crying. The women are adding their sobs to the plaintive exhortations of the wounded. All the time the shelling never abates. The arena of the defenders is veneered. Nearly every man, woman and child is lyddite-stained. The muddy stream is yellow. The night was an awful one. For two days the men are without food, but worse still are the pestiferous air, the loathsome water, and the suffering of the wounded. It is too much for flesh and blood. The morning of the 27th February saw the first white flag hoisted by a Boer general. It was a woeful sight when 3600 Boers, undisciplined peasants, reluctantly threw down their rifles among the wreck of the shells and ambled past the English lines. They had withstood the onslaught of 80,000 British troops with modern death-dealing implements of war, and, towards the end of the siege, about 1000 guns were brought to bear upon them."

How far this disaster can be attributed to General Cronje is difficult to say. The following considerations may, however, throw some light on its causes.

During the early part of the war we hardly realised the great value and necessity of good scouting. It was only after General Cronje and his men had fallen into the hands of the enemy that a regular scouting corps was organised and placed under the control of the brave Danie Therou.

Lord Roberts's forces were almost on Cronje's laager before they were perceived, and unfortunately they were even then entirely under-estimated and consequently thought light of. Flushed by the victory at Magersfontein, the General did not contemplate the possibility of such a bitter reverse. He was going to strike another hard blow at the enemy—he did strike it, but at too great a cost. Had he realised his position the first or second day after the siege was begun, he might still have escaped. The convoy would have been captured, but the men would have been saved. The old gentleman was determined to hold all, and consequently lost all.

So far the General deserves censure and is accountable for the disaster which had such a far-reaching and bad moral effect on the rest of the burghers. The only sweet drop contained in the bitter cup extended to us was the fact that Cronje and his burghers surrendered *as men*, and not as *cowards*. Once surrounded and brought to bay they resisted every attack with admirable fortitude and valour. Surrounded along the banks of the Modder River, at a spot where they had no cover at all, exposed to a terrific cannonade and charged by thousands of the enemy from time to time, these farmers fearlessly repelled every onslaught. It was one thing to surround them, another thing to capture them. They were not to be taken with cold hands. The enemy, especially the Canadians, had to pay a great price before the white flag announced Cronje's unconditional surrender.

During the siege attempts were made by General De Wet to relieve Cronje, but none succeeded. Several of the relieving forces, including the pick of the Winburg Commando with Commandant Theunissen, were themselves surrounded and captured in trying to break through the lines of the besiegers.

To intensify the gloom, Ladysmith, which was daily expected to fall, was relieved on the day of Cronje's surrender. For certain reasons the late Commandant-General P. Joubert had evacuated the positions round Ladysmith and retreated to the Biggar's Range. General Louis Botha, who was engaging Buller's relieving forces at Colenso, was then also compelled to retreat.

After Cronje's capture the way to Bloemfontein and Pretoria lay open. The Boers made one more stand at Abraham's

Kraal, where the enemy suffered heavily, but carried the day by their overwhelming numbers. After the British occupied Bloemfontein the Transvaal burghers became reluctant to offer battle in the Free State, on the ground that there were no positions from which they could successfully check the ever-advancing foe. Many of the Free Staters were discouraged and hopeless; but rest renewed their strength and zeal, and they shortly returned to the struggles.

The second disaster which befell the two Republics was the ignominious and cowardly surrender of Prinsloo, which took place on the 1st of August, 1900. For various reasons this surrender was more keenly felt by the Boers than that of Cronje. The one, though he might have blundered, nevertheless acted the part of a brave, though obstinate, man; the other that of a coward.

Some six weeks after the occupation of Bloemfontein the British troops resumed their northward march, and so quickly did they advance, almost day and night, that Pretoria was soon occupied. What this rapid movement meant, we could not quite understand. Did Lord Roberts think that the occupation of Pretoria would terminate hostilities? The British forces in their swift march to the Transvaal capital left Free State burghers behind them as they advanced. These men rallied again under General De Wet and seriously threatened the English line of communications, capturing seven hundred of the British at Roode Wal.

Large forces under Hector MacDonald and Bruce Hamilton recrossed the Vaal in order to crush the Free Staters. Then Prinsloo surrendered. Having accompanied the commandos that surrendered under him, we will relate the story of that most sad incident of the War.

On the occupation of Bethlehem by the British in the

beginning of July, 1900, the Boer commandos, under General De Wet, retreated to the Wittebergen, a mountain range to the south-east of Bethlehem, forming a semi-circle round Fouriesburg, a small village on the Basutoland border. This range, with its towering peaks and steep slopes, formed an impregnable stronghold. The burghers thought that, once behind those heaven-high mountains, with all the passes in their possession, with abundant war supplies, and all the necessaries of life, they would resist successfully every attack. The camps were pitched at the base of the mountains. The burghers began at once to make turf-bulwarks for the guns, and trenches for themselves, in the various passes.

General De Wet, who did not seem quite at ease in this enclosure or kraal, for such it was, organised the Bethlehem-Heilbron burghers into a commando 2500 strong and left with these in the direction of Heilbron. General Roux from Senekal was instructed to organise another commando, 1000 or 1200 strong, and advance with that in the direction of Bloemfontein. For some reason or other, General Roux's departure was delayed, and so he with all his men fell into Prinsloo's meshes.

On Monday, 23rd July, the enemy made a general attack on all the Boer positions, except Naauwpoort Pass. These attacks, though very determined, were unsuccessful. From sunrise to sunset the firing never ceased. The burghers in Slabberts Nek, where we happened to be, were subjected to a dreadful cannon fire. This pass was guarded by Captain Smith with two Krupp guns and Lieutenant Carlblom with a pom-pom. Upon these guns the English directed two Howitzers and six Armstrongs. Here, just before sunset, the gallant Captain Rautenbagh was blown to pieces by a lyddite shell, which exploded in front of him.

Thus repulsed by day, the enemy succeeded in scaling the

heights to the left of the Boers at Slabberts Nek by an unguarded footpath during the night. As soon as the crimson light of a July dawn had exposed the frost-covered ridges, the dark overcoats on the left of the Boer positions revealed the unwelcome fact that the enemy had gained their object of the day before, and had outflanked the Boers.

Not only at Slabberts Nek, but also at Reliefs Nek the Boers were outflanked the same night. At the latter pass a number of Highlanders had occupied the rocky heights during the stillness of the night, so that when the Boer pickets discovered them the next morning they found the enemy commanding a position higher than their own, which they forthwith abandoned. The enemy, now in possession of two mountain passes, forced the Boers to evacuate all the other passes, by threatening an attack on our rear and surrounding us. So on Tuesday morning, at about 9 A.M., the commandos quitted the mountains and fell back on Fouriesburg.

Our situation was becoming hourly more and more embarrassing. There was just one thing to be done, and that was to move as quickly as possible all along the base of the mountain range, and to seize a pass called Naauwpoort Nek farther northwards. That pass was not yet occupied by the enemy, and there it was possible to secure a safe exit; and higher up the mountain range, at the farm of Salmon Raads, was another pass which could be reached in due time.

If Prinsloo had, in his heart, desired to save his commandos, he could have done so easily. But no sooner had we left the mountains than we noticed that strange whispers were passed from man to man; we heard it said that a further prolongation of the war was absolutely useless; that many of the officers and burghers were tired of it, and would like to go home. In short, we saw what was coming, and anticipated the surrender.

When the commandos arrived at Naauwpoort Pass they found their exit cut off there by the enemy. Instead of hastening on to the next pass, the officers held a council of war to discuss the situation, or, more correctly, to deliberate on a surrender. The meeting lasted almost all night. Some of the officers were deadly opposed to a surrender; others—and they were the majority—were in favour of it. Nothing, however, was decided at that meeting, for a Hoofd Commandant had first to be elected before any steps could be taken.

A second meeting of officers for the purpose of electing a Chief Commandant was next held. In that meeting Prinsloo was elected Chief Commandant, but, as not all the officers were present, some of them being still in the positions, it was beforehand agreed that the man elected by that meeting should have no authority before the votes of the absent officers were taken, and when their votes came in it was found that General Roux, and not Prinsloo, was elected.

The latter, however, entered into negotiations with the enemy before this question as to whom was to be Chief Commandant was settled. He first asked for an armistice, which was refused. Then he asked for terms, to which General Hunter replied: "Unconditional surrender is demanded." Prinsloo, well aware that the burghers would not surrender unconditionally, pleaded and insisted on terms.

At this juncture Vilonel, the deserter, who had been sentenced for five years' imprisonment for high treason, but who was, unfortunately, released, appeared on the scene. He came from the British lines, met Prinsloo, and officiated as intermediary between Generals Hunter and Prinsloo. Something in the shape of terms was drawn up, but these terms, if tested and analysed, amounted to unconditional surrender. As soon as Prinsloo was in possession of these conditions, he forwarded a report to the different commandants that he had been successful in obtaining good terms from the English, and that they must evacuate their positions so as to arrange for a surrender. This report was sent on to Commandant Potgieter of Smithfield with instructions to forward it to the next commandant.

General Roux, on learning of Prinsloo's doings, at once dispatched a report to the different commandos notifying to them that Prinsloo had no right to negotiate with the enemy, to ask for or accept terms for a surrender. Also, that the burghers must on no account abandon their positions. He, so the report ran, would personally go to protest against the illegal surrender. The General went, but did not return. Why he went himself, and did not send one of his adjutants with a written protest, seems still very strange to us. He was warned not to go. General Fourie's last words to him were: "Good-bye, General; I greet you, never to see you again in the Boer ranks." He did not heed the warning, and so we lost one of our bravest and best leaders.

Unfortunately, General Roux's report fell into the hands of Commandant Potgieter, who, siding with Prinsloo on the question of a surrender, had it destroyed whilst Prinsloo's was forwarded. This settled the whole affair. The positions were evacuated, and in part occupied by the enemy. Still, at the eleventh hour, there was a possibility of escape. The long trail of waggons would have been captured, but most, if not all, the burghers could have found their way out. But no, they were to be duped by a set of unscrupulous officers. They were told they could get all they desired, except their independence. All could go home, each would get a horse-saddle and bridle, their private property would not be confiscated, and they would be allowed to follow their agricultural and pastoral pursuits undisturbed. And the poor officers—well for them that there were no extenuating terms, no mercy. So, at least, said Commandant Polly de Villiers, of the Ficksburg Commando. He, when posing as a martyr, announced these conditions to the burghers, who, after such long separation from their families, found it impossible to withstand such charming terms. Sorrowfully were they disillusioned after they had laid down their arms.

To make the surrender a complete success, all sorts of rumours were freely circulated. The burghers were told that all who did not surrender would be shot as rebels when captured, that the pass, higher up the mountains, was guarded by twenty-five lyddite guns, so that every exit was cut off by the enemy. When these reports were brought to bear on men already depressed and discouraged it did not require great pressure to effect their surrender. Still, if these men had not been misled, if they had known that Ceylon and India would be the final destination of many of them, they never would have surrendered, and very few of them would have been captured there and then. All this they found out when it was too late.

These unfortunate burghers we do not wish to criticise too severely. The officers were to blame. Many of them certainly fell into the hands of the enemy through no fault of their own. There were, however, some who were only too ready to lay down their arms, and these were the majority. They did not act the part of men; for they deserted shamefully those who still struggled bravely for freedom. Nor am I willing to judge these. Let conscience speak to such as these.

Some officers, animated by a truer love of their country, protested strongly against such an illegal and shameful surrender. One of these, General Olivier of the Rouxville Commando, called his burghers together and told them plainly what he thought. He warned them not to place too much credence in British promises, and promised that those who would follow him he would lead out safely. Of his whole commando—about four hundred strong—scarcely seventy followed him. The others surrendered.

Besides attending to his men, General Olivier also took charge of most of the Boer guns, which were to have formed no mean part of the booty, for Prinsloo had promised the British some thirteen guns, one pom-pom, and a few maxims with all their ammunition. In the pass at Salmon Raads, General Hector MacDonald met Olivier with the guns. He at once ordered him to go no farther, as he was a surrendered man. Olivier tarried as long as it pleased him, and then proceeded, taking the guns along with him.

Of all the Boer forces concentrated in the Wittebergen, only about six hundred did not surrender. To secure these also every means were resorted to. No fewer than three times were messengers sent to them with reports from the enemy. At first we were courteously invited to return and surrender. To prove to us the validity of the surrender, all the papers bearing on the negotiation from first to last were forwarded to us. The excellent conditions granted to the surrendered burghers were also transmitted to us. In these conditions we observed that the surrendered burghers would each be provided with a horse to ride to their destination, which would be Winburg, till further orders. We saw also that they would be kept as prisoners-of-war until the war was over, which meant, though they did not suspect it then, two years longer. Their private property was to be respected. How the last condition was violated is well known.

Olivier and his men were, however, not to be easily ensnared. He politely rejected the proffered terms, stating at the same time that Prinsloo's surrender was illegal. A few days later, and lo! in the distance we beheld another flag-of-truce, a second report. The polite request had failed, intimidation must now be tried—that might succeed better.

We were admonished urgently to come back at once, and surrender without further delay. Failing that, we must not expect to receive such generous and lenient treatment as would be extended to those surrendered already. All our goods would be confiscated, etc.

On receiving this report, Olivier sent back the somewhat curt and abrupt reply: "That if the British wanted his rifle they would have to capture him as a man, for he would not surrender like an old woman. And he would receive no more white flags on this matter." Consequently the third messenger was sent back without being interviewed.

So much for the Prinsloo disaster. It was a sad one for those still struggling against overwhelming odds. Many a heart beat low, and many a sigh was heaved. That was an "unkind cut," which wounded the hearts of thousands. Many a one, even of those who stood to the last day, never recovered from the effects of that shock. They fought bravely, and did their duty towards their country, but hope for an ultimate victory was dead within them.

And those who surrendered, what lessons they had to learn! Even to-day, a year after the close of the war, some of them have not reached their homes, but are on lonely islands, and in distant India, while many have passed away to the unseen world on those foreign shores. Those that came back, what did they find? A country strewn with ruins, their homes destroyed and burnt, and their sheep and cattle stabbed and shot lying in heaps upon the ground. What a sad sight did greet their eyes! How many of their beloved families were missing, having died in the Concentration Camps. But when they reflect on the past the saddest thought should be their vanished freedom.

The next ordeal through which the Republicans had to pass

began with the denudation of the two States. As arms alone could not subdue the Boers, some other expedient had to be tried—the starvation process was resorted to; all food-stuff had to be destroyed or removed, so that the burghers should not obtain sustenance. The country had to be cleared of cattle and sheep—in fact, of everything which could keep the Boers alive. This was considered the most feasible way of defeating the so-called *marauding* bands of armed Boers.

But what about the women-folk, if the country is to be cleared? Well, these must go to Concentration Camps, from which so many never returned. We do not wish to dwell on the sufferings of Boer women and children; but what we are proud to note is that when military operations were conducted against the weak and defenceless, the burgher was touched to the centre of his heart. Call a Boer by what name you please, but of this be assured—he is a man who, above all, loves his family, and has pride and pleasure in his home, be it never so humble. When, therefore, a destructive policy was adopted, who shall realise fully what passed through the minds of these as they stood watching the lurid flames of their burning homes, and heard how in the camps their families were dying in scores? Cronje's capture, Prinsloo's surrender, and all the hard fighting they had to do, seemed but trifles as compared to this, by far the saddest, phase of the South African War.

Another dark day, and the curtain drops. We refer to that day when the documents were signed and peace was concluded. Then, indeed, the darkness seemed tangible Who shall number the tears shed on that day—tears of men, women, and even children? Tears of men who had fought for almost three years, who had sacrificed their all, who had but one object in view, one ideal to pursue; who loved liberty and independence, with an amazing love. Tears of women, who had spent many months either in camps, or in the open veldt;

women whose husbands and sons had fallen in the war, whose infants were laid low in many a graveyard. Tears of children, who had lost their parents, children who never more would know the love of a mother, the protection of a father. With one voice the whole people lamented the loss of their beloved Fatherland.

And how did the officers who had to subscribe to these terms of peace feel? Let one[A] who was present speak:

> "Never shall I forget what I witnessed there. General De Wet showed that there was no chance any longer of continuing the struggle ... I see him yet, that unyielding man, with his piercing eyes, his strong mouth and chin—I see him there still, like a lion fallen into a snare. He will not, he cannot, but he must give up the struggle! I still see the stern faces of the officers, who up to that moment had been so unbending. I see them staring as if into empty space. I see engraved upon their faces an indescribable expression, an expression that seemed to ask: 'Is this the bitter end of our sufferings and our sorrows, of our faith and our strong crying to God?' How great was their emotion! I saw the lips of men quiver who had never trembled before a foe. I saw tears brimming in eyes that had been dry when they had seen their dearest laid in the grave....
>
> "Everything was as silent as death when acting President Burger took the pen in his hand. I looked at my watch; it was five minutes past eleven on the 31st day of May in the year 1902.
>
> "President Burger signed. President Steyn was not there. Our hearts bled at the thought that he had been seized by a dangerous malady; and yet it seemed to me that something was owed to that malady, since it prevented the

> President of the Orange Free State from doing what would have caused him the greatest pain in the world. He had said once: 'To set my hand to a paper to sign away the Independence of my people—that I shall never do.' Sad circumstances, which he might then almost have called fortunate, had brought it about that what he would not do, that he could not do. The document was signed! All were silent in that room where so much had been spoken."

We quote the terms of peace in full:—

> "His Excellency General Lord Kitchener, and His Excellency Lord Milner, on behalf of the British Government, and Messrs. M.T. Steyn, J. Brebner, General C.R. De Wet, General C. Olivier, and Judge J.B.M. Hertzog, acting as the Government of the Orange Free State, and Messrs. S.W. Burger, F.W. Reitz, Generals Louis Botha, J.H. de la Rey, Lucas Meyer, and C. Krogh, acting as the Government of the South African Republic, on behalf of their respective burghers, desirous to terminate the present hostilities, agree on the following articles:—
>
> "I. The burgher forces in the field will forthwith lay down their arms, handing over all guns, rifles, and munitions of war in their possession or under their control, and desist from any further resistance to the authority of His Majesty King Edward VII., whom they recognise as their lawful Sovereign. The manner and details of this surrender will be arranged between Lord Kitchener and Commandant-General Botha, Assistant Commandant-General Delarey, and Chief Commandant De Wet.
>
> "2. All burghers in the field outside the limits of the Transvaal or Orange River Colony, and all prisoners of war at present outside South Africa, who are burghers, will, on duly declaring their acceptance of the position of

subjects of His Majesty King Edward VII., be gradually brought back to their homes as soon as transport can be provided and their means of subsistence ensured.

"3. The burghers so surrendering or so returning will not be deprived of their personal liberty or their property.

"4. No proceedings, civil or criminal, will be taken against any of the burghers so surrendering or so returning for any acts in connection with the prosecution of the war. The benefit of this clause will not extend to certain acts contrary to the usage of war which have been notified by the Commander-in-Chief to the Boer Generals and which shall be tried by court-martial immediately after the close of hostilities.

"5. The Dutch language will be taught in public schools in the Transvaal and Orange River Colony where the parents of the children desire it, and will be allowed in courts of law when necessary for the better and more effectual administration of justice.

"6. The possession of rifles will be allowed in the Transvaal and Orange River Colony to persons requiring them for their protection, on taking out a licence according to law.

"7. Military administration in the Transvaal and Orange River Colony will at the earliest possible date be succeeded by Civil Government, and, as soon as circumstances permit, representative institutions, leading up to self-government, will be introduced.

"8. The question of granting the franchise to natives will not be decided until after the introduction of self-government.

"9. No special tax will be imposed on landed property in the Transvaal and Orange River Colony to defray the expenses of the War.

"10. As soon as conditions permit, a Commission, on which the local inhabitants will be represented, will be appointed in each district of the Transvaal and Orange River Colony, under the presidency of a Magistrate or other official, for the purpose of assisting the restoration of the people to their homes, and supplying those who, owing to war losses, are unable to provide for themselves, with food, shelter, and the necessary amount of seed, stock, implements, etc., indispensable to the resumption of their normal occupations. His Majesty's Government will place at the disposal of these Commissions a sum of three million pounds sterling for the above purposes, and will allow all notes issued under Law No. I, of 1900, of the South African Republic, and all receipts given by officers in the field of the late Republics, or under their orders, to be presented to a Judicial Commission, which will be appointed by the Government; and if such notes and receipts are found by this Commission to have been duly issued in return for valuable considerations, they will be received by the first named Commissions as evidence of war losses suffered by the persons to whom they were originally given. In addition to the above named free grant of three million pounds, His Majesty's Government will be prepared to make advances on loan for the same purposes, free of interest for two years, and afterwards repayable over a period of three years with three per cent. interest. No foreigner or rebel will be entitled to the benefit of this clause."

Statement read by Lord Milner to the Boer delegates:—

"His Majesty's Government must place it on record that

the treatment of Cape and Natal Colonists who have been in rebellion, and who now surrender, will, if they return to their Colonies, be determined by the Colonial Governments, and in accordance with the laws of the Colonies, and that any British subjects who have joined the enemy will be liable to trial under the law of that part of the British Empire to which they belong.

"His Majesty's Government are informed by the Cape Government that the following are their views as to the terms which should be granted to British subjects of Cape Colony who are now in the field, or who have surrendered, or have been captured since the 12th of April, 1901: With regard to rank and file, that they should all, upon surrender, after giving up their arms, sign a document before the Resident Magistrate of the District in which the surrender takes place, acknowledging themselves guilty of High Treason, and that the punishment to be awarded to them, provided they shall not have been guilty of murder, or other acts contrary to the usages of civilised warfare, should be that they shall not be entitled for life to be registered as voters, or to vote at any Parliamentary Divisional Council, or Municipal election.

"With reference to Justices of the Peace and Field Cornets of the Cape Colony, and all other persons holding an official position under the Government of the Cape Colony, or who may occupy the position of Commandant of rebel or burgher forces, they should be tried for High Treason before the ordinary court of the country, or such special court as may be hereafter constituted by Law, the punishment for their offence to be left to the discretion of the Court, with this proviso, that in no case shall the penalty of Death be inflicted.

"The Natal Government are of opinion that rebels should

be dealt with according to the Law of the Colony."

To the Boer, although he had been suffering the manifold miseries of the battlefield for over two years, such terms made peace a tragedy. Bitterness was mixed with his cup of happiness when he found himself once more united to his family.

[Footnote A: Rev. Kestell, 'Through Shot and Flames.']

CHAPTER III

ENGAGEMENTS

And in the hope of freedom they possess
All that the contest calls for,—spirit, strength,
The scorn of danger, and united hearts.

—*Cowper*

With the exception of the Stormberg engagement we do not intend to dwell on the battles of the first part of the campaign. They have already been described by able hands, by men who participated in them, or were in a position to ascertain their true history. By this we do not infer that all accounts are correct, for it requires many eyes to see one battle in all its aspects. Besides, some writers are unconsciously influenced and prejudiced by their national sentiments, and thus fail to do justice to the parties concerned. We shall confine ourselves to the engagements in which we personally took part, and shall record only the more remarkable among them.

BATTLE OF STORMBERG.

In the beginning of November, 1899, the commandoes of Rouxville, Smithfield, and Bethulie entered the Cape Colony at different points. Having occupied several villages in the Eastern Province, they concentrated towards the end of the month in the Stormbergen. Our tents were pitched on the northern slopes of this mountain range, which runs from east to west, six miles to the north of Molteno. Here we were to have our first lesson in actual fighting; for up to that time we had not encountered any resistance on the part of the enemy.

On the 9th of December, the night fixed on by General Gatacre to strike a blow at the Boer forces at Stormberg, Assistant Chief Commandant Grobler left that place with about nine hundred burghers, intending to occupy Steynsburg. The enemy, having heard of their departure, and knowing that our positions were in consequence so much weaker, left that same evening, fully resolved to surprise us, and, if possible, reoccupy the Stormbergen, which were abandoned at the first approach of our commandoes.

The object of the British was to attack us on our right flank before dawn, seize our positions and force us to surrender or retreat. On paper this plan presented no difficulties, but its accomplishment was not quite so easy, and proved a dangerous operation. The English general, as we afterwards learnt, had started for the Boer positions at too late an hour to reach them in due time; and, moreover, had lost his way in the darkness of the night, so that the first rays of the rising sun were lighting the majestic mountain tops before he was in position.

The "brandwachten"—night pickets—of the Rouxville Commando were already on their way back to the camp, when one of them, who had by chance returned to the top of the mountain, saw, in the shadow of the valley, and on the slopes of the mountain, human forms moving silently onward. One glance of his keen eye assured him that those forms were enemies. Bang! went the first rifle report. The other pickets all rushed back and opened fire as swiftly as they could handle their Mausers. This brought the enemy to a standstill, for they, too, were surprised.

In the Boer camp below some of us were still peacefully sleeping, while others were enjoying their first cup of coffee. With the rifle reports came wakefulness and bustle. It did not take us a moment to realise that speed would be our only means of salvation. Should the enemy reach the summit first, disaster and defeat would be our lot. For some minutes it was a scene of confusion. The horses, saddles, bridles, rifles and bandoliers, where were they? Some knew, and had their equipments ready in a moment; others, less careful, did not know, and sought almost frantically for theirs. We made for the mountain and scaled it as swiftly as our feet could carry us. Exhausted and breathless we reached the summit before the enemy.

Gatacre's men were now exposed to a somewhat confused fire, which greatly embarrassed them. Subjected to this fire from the summit, some concealed themselves behind the rocks, while others retreated for shelter to a donga not far off.

The English battery was then brought into action, and opened a terrific fire on our positions, commanded by only two Krupp guns. So unceasing and accurate was the enemy's fire, that our guns were soon silenced. In a short time some of our burghers fell wounded and a few killed. One of the enemy's guns was taken by mistake too near to our positions, with the result that, in a few minutes, all its horses and most of the gunners were disabled, and the gun passed into our hands.

Although exposed to a violent bombardment, we held our ground and repelled the repeated attacks of Gatacre's men, who began to realise that, should their guns not speedily dislodge us, the attack was bound to collapse.

After the engagement had lasted an hour and a half we noticed that the enemy began to waver, and was planning a retreat. To their dismay General Grobler now made his appearance with reinforcements. He had encamped that night some nine miles from Stormberg, and on hearing the report of the guns, returned with Commandant du Plooy of Bethulie to assist the Stormberg defenders.

On his arrival the enemy, exposed to a cross-fire, ran the risk of being surrounded and captured. There was but one way out of a wretched position—one loophole out of the net. Fortunately for them, Commandant Zwanepoel of Smithfield, who had just given orders to guard this way of escape, was badly wounded while rising to lead on his men. Owing to this mishap his burghers failed to carry out his instructions, thus leaving the way open.

Gatacre, seeing that it was a hopeless struggle, abandoned the project of reoccupying Stormberg and sounded the retreat. He was followed up for some distance by Commandant du Plooy, who made a few prisoners and took two ammunition waggons. Weary and thirsty, the English forces re-entered Molteno that evening. They had been baffled in a determined attack. Their losses amounted to about 700, captured, wounded and killed. Those who had taken shelter behind the rocks and in the donga were all made prisoners. They remained there till the rest had retreated, and then hoisted the white flag. One English writer says that they were shamefully forgotten by General Gatacre, who was thus responsible for their loss. Indeed a questionable explanation! Among the wounded were a few officers and some privates, who were seriously injured by their own guns as they tried to seize the Boer positions. Colonel Eagar, one of the wounded, was removed to our hospital, where he breathed his last. In addition to the number of prisoners we also captured two big guns. Our losses amounted to 6 killed and 27 wounded.

The attack on the Stormberg positions, if it was boldly conceived, was badly carried out. The English general should have postponed the attack when it dawned upon him that he would not reach the enemy's positions before daybreak; and he should have used the knowledge, common to most soldiers, that it is best to attack a foe's weakest side. This was not done at Stormberg. We, too, suffered from ill-advised action—or rather, inaction. For we had had the opportunity of capturing, if not all, most of Gatacre's men, with all their guns, and we neglected it! The victory would have been complete if we had only followed up our advantage. In those early days, however, some of our leaders regarded it as rather sinful to harass a retreating enemy.

SANNA'S POST.

On the occupation of Bloemfontein some of the burghers, discouraged and despondent, left for their homes. Lord Roberts's proclamation, promising protection to all who should lay down their arms and settle quietly on their farms, enticed many to remain at home. Most, however, changed their minds after a few weeks' rest and returned to their commandoes.

It was then, after they had rallied again, that General De Wet, on the eve of the 28th of March, left Brandfort with a commando 1500 strong and moved in the direction of Winburg. De Wet had made up his mind to surprise the English garrison which guarded the Bloemfontein Waterworks at Sanna's Post, and so cut off the water supply of Bloemfontein.

With that object in view he made his movements thither by night, so as to keep the enemy in the dark as to his plans. Neither were these disclosed to the burghers, who were naturally anxious to know where they were going and what they were to do next.

On his way De Wet learnt that General Broadwood, dreading an attack of Commandant Olivier, had quitted Ladybrand and was marching on Bloemfontein with a strong force. This information was rather disconcerting, for now he had not only to reckon with the garrison, but to be ready for an engagement with a column 2000 strong, which might come to the relief of the garrison at any moment. In case of such an emergency, De Wet divided his forces into two parts. He placed one division—1050 strong with four guns—under the control of Generals Cronje, Froneman, Wessels, and Piet De Wet, with instructions to occupy the positions east of the Modder River and directly opposite the Waterworks, so as to check Broadwood, should he come to the rescue of the garrison.

Taking the remaining 350 burghers he set out to Koorn Spruit, a brook which flows into the Modder River. Arrived there, he carefully concealed his horses and men at a point where the road from the Waterworks to Bloemfontein passes through the brook. The other generals were to shell the garrison at daybreak, while he would fall on the troops if they tried to escape to Bloemfontein *via* Koorn Spruit.

As the Boer forces were getting into their different positions during the night, Broadwood, who had left Thaba 'Nchu at nightfall, arrived that very night at Sanna's Post. But we were each unconscious of the other's presence.

The next morning at daybreak we saw a waggon and a large number of cattle and sheep not far off the brook. The Kaffir drivers informed us that the British column had just arrived at Sanna's Post. As soon as we could see some distance ahead, we observed the enemy now hardly 3000 paces off. A few minutes later our guns began to play upon the unsuspecting British forces. What a scene of confusion! Broadwood had fallen into a trap and was between two fires. The whole column, with guns, waggons and carts, made hurriedly for the drift where De Wet and his men lay hidden. Nearer they came. At length a cart entered the drift. The occupants, husband and wife, looked bewildered on seeing armed Boers all around them in the bed of the brook. De Wet immediately ordered two of his adjutants to mount the cart and drive on. Then in quick succession followed a number of carts and vehicles, all driven by Englishmen from Thaba 'Nchu. These were ordered to proceed ahead and warned not to make any signals to the enemy. So well was everything arranged, that the first batch of troops that entered the drift had not the slightest suspicion that there was something wrong. Absolutely abashed were they on finding themselves among us; the men raised their hands in surrender at the cry of "Hands up!"

In this way we disarmed 200 without wasting a bullet. But this was not to go on for long; there came an officer from the rear who was determined to upset our plans and disturb our peace seriously. He, at least, was not going to surrender in this fashion. On being asked for his rifle he said, with marked resoluteness, "Be d—d! I won't," and called on his men to fire. He drew his sword, but before he could use it he was no more among the living.

The battle had begun. Scarcely 100 paces from the banks of the brook stood five of the enemy's guns and more than 100 waggons. Some 400 paces from these two more guns had stopped. The enemy had withdrawn for cover about 1300 yards to the station on the Dewetsdorp-Bloemfontein railway.

It was while they were retreating to this station that the greatest havoc was wrought among them. Across the open plain, with no cover at all, they had to retreat, and before they reached the place of shelter the ground between the brook and the station was thickly strewn with their dead and wounded. It was, indeed, a ghastly scene. The burghers stood erect and fired on the retreating foe as though they were so much game. So quickly did the waggons and guns wheel round that many were overturned. To remove them was impossible. In vain did the English try to save the guns. They succeeded, however, in getting two to the station house, where they had rallied. With these they bombarded us for some time; but owing to our sheltered positions only two men were wounded.

The Boer forces on the east of the Modder River had in the meanwhile been doing their best to come to the assistance of General De Wet. But their progress was much retarded by the uneven veldt and dongas through which they had to ride. After three hours, spent in fruitless attempts, they forded the river, attacked the enemy with great energy, and succeeded in putting them to flight, and this brought the battle to an end.

We made 480 captives. What their losses in wounded and killed were is difficult to estimate. In the evening, when all was over, we went to the house where the wounded were gathered, and there counted in one room alone 96 cases. Their own report made their losses 350 dead and wounded. Besides, 7 guns and 117 waggons fell into our hands. Our loss consisted in 3 killed and 5 wounded.

On looking at the bodies of the dead and listening to the groanings of the wounded, one was forced to say what a pity that the trap was discovered, that one brave man, through his very bravery, prevented the bloodless capture of his column and his general.

MOSTERT'S HOEK.

The victory at Sanna's Post was soon followed up by another success over the British arms. On the evening of the eventful day at the Waterworks De Wet handed the command over to Generals A. Cronje and Piet De Wet, and, having taken three of his staff, he went in the direction of Dewetsdorp on a reconnoitring expedition.

The following day he learnt that a party of the enemy had occupied Dewetsdorp. On receiving the report his mind was made up: these too must be captured. He was then thirty miles away from the commandoes, but instantly despatched a report to us to come post-haste so as to attack the enemy at Dewetsdorp or intercept them, should they try to join the main body, which was advancing under Gatacre on Reddersburg.

In the meanwhile the burghers of that district, who had gone to their farms on the fall of Bloemfontein, were commandeered. With these, some 120, who were almost all unarmed, De Wet started for Dewetsdorp to watch the movements of the British.

Early on the 2nd of April the enemy left Dewetsdorp, and resumed their march to Reddersburg. While marching De Wet kept them all the while under surveillance. He was moving on one of their flanks, parallel to them with an intervening distance of six miles. They were evidently not aware that he was so close to them. As soon as we received the report concerning the British, we left Sanna's Post in haste. We required no urging on. For were we not encouraged by our recent success, and was there not every chance of achieving another? We left Sanna's Post a little before sunset, and that whole night we rode on without off-saddling once. We did not halt save for a few minutes to rest our horses.

Early the following morning a third report, pressing us to increase our speed and leave behind those whose horses were too tired to proceed rapidly, reached us. De Wet was most anxious to occupy a ridge in front of the enemy, between the farms Mostert's Hoek and Sterkfontein. The road leading to Reddersburg from Dewetsdorp traverses this ridge. Hence it was absolutely necessary to seize it before the enemy if we were to intercept them.

So on we went, leaving the weary and exhausted behind to follow on as soon as possible. About 9 A.M. Generals Froneman and De Villiers, with 350 men, met De Wet, who was still moving parallel to the British column, obscured from their view by a rising of the ground.

The ridge referred to already loomed now in the distance. We were all fiercely anxious to seize it before the enemy. For it was a question of life and death who was to be first there. But our horses were too tired, and began to fall out rapidly. We were still four miles from the ridge when the English began to occupy the eastern extremity of it. We moved on to the western extremity, and reached it in time.

The enemy, however, had the advantage of the best positions, but was fortunately cut off from the water. We were resolved to hem them in completely, for we knew that, if no relieving forces arrived, they would be compelled by thirst alone, if nothing else, to surrender.

Before commencing the fight, De Wet, anxious as usual to avoid unnecessary bloodshed, sent the following note to the commanding officer:—

"SIR,—I am here with 500 men, and am every moment

> expecting reinforcements with three Krupps, against which you will not be able to hold out. I therefore advise you, in order to prevent bloodshed, to surrender."

The messenger returned under a storm of bullets, for no sooner had he left the English lines than they opened fire on him. How he was missed seemed inexplicable. The answer he brought back was: "I am d—d if I surrender." On receiving this reply firing at once commenced. Positions nearer to the enemy were gradually occupied.

Towards sunset our guns arrived, and were brought to bear upon the enemy. But darkness soon set in, and firing ceased on both sides. To make sure that the enemy would not escape during the night, we occupied positions all round them, and in the darkness of the night silently stole as near to their positions as was possible.

The next morning, as soon as the glimmer of dawn revealed the Mauser sights to our eyes, the firing started with renewed vigour. We had drawn so close to the enemy that when our guns were brought in action we could, under cover of these, storm their positions. The men boldly rushed up to the enemy's skanzes, and some burghers even seized their rifles by the barrels, as they presented these over the bulwarks, calling out, "Hands up! hands up!"

At 11 A.M. the white flag was hoisted. The commanding officer, who had refused to surrender, was mortally wounded. Three hundred and seventy were sent to the Transvaal as prisoners-of-war, while their wounded and killed numbered 92.

Among the English we found five Boer prisoners-of-war, who were likewise exposed to our firing. Imagine their joy in being released! They greeted us with the ejaculation: "Thank

God we are free!" We mourned the death of Veldt Cornet du Plessis of Kroonstad, who fell after the white flag had been hoisted. That such mistakes should occur! Six or seven burghers were wounded.

LADYBRAND VISITED.

Towards the end of July, 1900, Prinsloo's surrender took place. Those of us who escaped the trap laid left for Heilbron with the hope of meeting De Wet's commando there. Near Heilbron we heard the dismal news that he was forced over the Vaal and was being driven northward by some 40,000 troops. This, led us to change our course and move in the direction of Winburg.

On the morning of the 27th of August we made an unsuccessful attack on Winburg. Olivier, with 27 men, got captured. The burden and responsibility of leading others was then first placed upon my shoulders. I was elected commandant.

Frustrated in our attempt to seize Winburg, we resolved to attack Ladybrand, which was not strongly garrisoned. Having encamped at Koeranerberg—a mountain 30 miles west of Ladybrand—we mustered our forces, took three guns and about 800 burghers, and left for the village.

It was a bitterly cold night—one of those nights which one can hardly forget. We rode till sunrise without off-saddling once. At 9 P.M. we halted to prepare a hasty supper. How we enjoyed that! A few days before, the enemy had unwillingly provided us with sugar, coffee, milk, butter and cheese. Owing to the intense cold the men that had no overcoats wrapped themselves up in their blankets, in which they appeared before the village just as the sun was rising.

Commandant Hertzog, on our arrival, despatched a messenger under a flag of truce to demand the surrender of the garrison. In reply he received a message to the effect that it would be much better if he would come in himself and lay down arms; that would put an end to the business much quicker. On receiving this answer we at once began to bombard the forts of the enemy, with the result that almost all their horses took to flight and fell into our hands, while some of them were wounded and killed.

General Fourie, Commandant Nieuwhoudt and myself, with a number of daring volunteers, made for the village. We reached a few houses safely, and under cover of these we succeeded in forcing the enemy to retreat to their forts and skanzes at the foot of Platrand—a mountain to the south-east of the village and very near to it. Gradually we occupied more and more of the village, and before sunset we were in possession of the whole of it.

The enemy was, however, so strongly entrenched that, in spite of their small numbers, it was impossible to compel them to capitulate without incurring the risk of sustaining heavy losses. For at the base of the mountain are natural forts and grottoes, against which lyddite shells would spend their force in vain. All we could do was to keep the foe in their haunts by directing such a fire against them that they could not venture even to peep out. In doing this the commandoes could requisition—loot, as some would say—what they required.

During the night the enemy shifted and occupied other positions. At daybreak they took vengeance on us from these positions. It did not take a long time to silence them for the rest of the day.

The following two days we remained in the village, keeping

the enemy at bay. We had hoped that eventually their rations would run short, and thus bring about their surrender. Unfortunately our hopes were not to be realised; they were only too well provided. Then, again, we thought that thirst might prove an irresistible force in our favour; but in this, too, we erred, for in their grottoes was abundant water.

On the second day of the attack we placed one of our guns in the centre of the village, whence we shelled the enemy's forts, but all to no purpose. On the evening of the third day we heard that relieving forces were at hand, and as we had received a message from De Wet to meet him in Bothaville district, we left Ladybrand at dusk.

During the three days' fighting only a few burghers were wounded. As the enemy fired at random into the village, some of the inhabitants were also injured. A young man was mortally wounded, while a bullet shattered the arm of a woman.

Our efforts were rewarded by the seizure of the enemy's horses, which we valued even more than their persons. The horses we could keep and use, the men we had to dismiss again. We returned to the laager well supplied with clothes and foodstuffs. But for some traitors, who assisted the enemy, the garrison would in all probability have fallen. These, dreading the results of a capitulation, held out until relieved.

As this was our first visit to Ladybrand since its occupation, the joy of the Boer families in meeting relatives and burghers was indeed great. They welcomed them with open arms, and during their short stay it was their delight to minister unto them. We shall ever gratefully remember the hearty reception which was extended to us by the Ladybrand Africanders. Were they not prosecuted after our departure for welcoming and receiving their kith and kin?

MURRAY'S COLUMN.

Compelled to abandon the Cape Colony in August, we went to Gastron District, a Free State village situated on the Basutoland border. There we intended to rest our horses for a time; but no sooner had we entered the district than the English column came pouring into it like so many birds of prey. They had concentrated in that district and in the adjoining ones to clear them, *i.e.*, to remove or destroy whatever could be removed or destroyed.

During this time we often came in conflict with the enemy. It was impossible to avoid that; they were on every side. For miles and miles it was one column on the other. We could hardly engage any of these columns successfully during the day, for no sooner had the fight begun than reinforcements would come from all directions, making our position quite untenable.

It was in such circumstances that we planned a night attack on one of the English camps nine miles east of Gastron. We had engaged the enemy on several occasions without desirable results. Our limited supply of ammunition was gradually exhausted. Come what would, we were bound to strike a blow at the enemy, so as to fill our bandoliers once more. The night was the only time we could hope to succeed. Reinforcements would not then scatter us before we had achieved our object.

At 11 P.M. on the 19th of September, 1901, after a day's hard fighting from early morn till sunset, we started, 70 men in all, with the intention of attacking a column encamped at the foot of a hill. It was a very cold night, and the moon, casting her pale light across the frosty plains, was sinking in the west. The column was about eight miles off. As we approached it, deep silence reigned. Not a word, not a whisper was heard. Ah! if we could but succeed in passing the enemy's pickets unobserved, the victory would be ours, the battle half won. So we held our breath and our tongues as well, and moved onward. Indeed, we have succeeded! We are past the pickets, and that unnoticed! The hill, where the slumbering foe is encamped, is in our possession.

Having dismounted, the burghers were arranged in fighting order. Commandant Louis Wessels was placed on one flank, Commandant De Bruijn on the other. Before commencing the work of destruction, we briefly admonished and encouraged the men to be true to each other and to fight as befits men. We pointed out to them that our success would depend entirely upon our united efforts. For a long address there was no time, so we proceeded to the camp.

The moon has set. Down below the enemy is fast asleep. Soon, too soon, their midnight slumbers will be sadly disturbed. Many of them will not see the dawn of another day. They are enjoying their last sleep.

Silently we moved on to the British column, which gave no signs whatever that our approach was suspected. As it was very dark, the men were ordered not to advance ahead of one another, for fear of accidents, and also, if possible, to march right through the camp, so as to make sure of all.

Commandant L. Wessels, famous for his dauntlessness, was the first to open fire by lodging a shot in one of the enemy's tents. The rest followed, and then a shower of bullets, thick and fast, poured in upon the surprised and embarrassed foe. The men aimed low and fired with deadly precision. The flashes of the rifles leapt forth like lightning freaks in the darkness. Never before had I witnessed such a scene.

In a quarter of an hour all was over and the whole camp taken. Two Maxims were destroyed and an Armstrong was taken along with us. What havoc was played in that brief quarter of an hour! The wounded mules, horses and men lay groaning side by side. Colonel Murray, Captain Murray, and almost all the other officers, fell in the action, and several privates passed into the unseen world that fatal night. So terrific was the firing that entire teams of mules were shot down where they stood tied to the ropes.

As the veldt was strewn with the many wounded and the dead, we could not put the waggons on fire, lest the grass should catch fire and consume the fallen in battle. We took what we could remove and left the camp—not exactly as we found it, but a little poorer.

The enemy, though attacked off their guard, defended themselves bravely. We shall not forget the gallant conduct of the officer who had charge of the Maxim. Distinctly we could hear him say, "Get the Maxim into action. Don't be afraid, boys. Go for them! Go for them!" Brave man! He, too, fell by the side of his Maxim, which was charged and seized by Commandant Wessels.

As to the conduct of the burghers, we need only remark that their good behaviour pleased us exceedingly. There was no reason to urge them on; not one retreated. Though only a handful as compared to the enemy, they fought well till the foe was vanquished. One of them, young Liebenberg (familiarly known by the name of Matie) from Murraysburg, was shot through the head and succumbed at once. Another, young Hugo from Smithfield, was wounded in the foot. We had no other casualties.

The attack on Murray's column was to a great extent incidental. Near his was another very much smaller camp.

When I left that night it was with the intention to attack this smaller camp, for I had only 65 men at my disposal. In the darkness I lost my way, and so lighted on Murray's column. It was unfortunate for them, but for ourselves we could have wished for no better accident.

In the Colonel's letter-bag we found a letter addressed to his wife, dated 19th September, 1901, and written the very day before his death. We purposed to forward that letter, but the following day the bag was retaken. Not only was it taken, but also the gun, while 20 burghers were captured and one—Myburgh—was killed. We were again surprised. Inconstant are the fortunes of war.

JAMES TOWN.

The villages in possession of the enemy were at length so thoroughly fortified that it was well-nigh impossible to seize them without sustaining great losses. Though they seemed impregnable, yet we were sometimes compelled by sheer necessity to attack them. Beyond expectation we now and again succeeded in inducing the garrison to surrender. Such was the case at James Town, a village in the Eastern Province of the Cape Colony.

Late one afternoon in the month of July, 1901, I set out to this village to reconnoitre it in person. Unobserved, I reached the summit of a small hill, about a mile from it. Through my field-glasses I carefully noted the various forts, and there and then planned an attack. The next morning I knew exactly what to do.

At 2 A.M. Commandant Myburgh, Commandant Loetter, and myself, with some 60 men, were in the saddle and on our way to James Town. What will be the issue? Shall we succeed? Can we surprise the enemy? Such questions we put to ourselves as we rode on in the darkness and silence of the night to accomplish the work of destruction.

The spot we had in view was a kopje, situated to the north of the village. Here the enemy's camp was located. As this kopje was the key to the village, it was necessarily very strongly fortified. We knew that if we could only occupy that hill, the rest would be easy work. Before dawn we were close to the camp. A few minutes more and we shall grimly salute our sleeping brethren. Silently we approach them. We are keenly on the alert for the pickets, whom, least of all, we wished to disturb. Behold! something in the darkness—what may that be? To be sure, two human forms! Hush! they are slumbering. Noiselessly we draw nearer, reach them, seize their rifles, and then—wake them. They are our first prisoners; our way to the camp is open, safe and sure.

On we moved until stopped, not by a sentinel—it was much too cold that night to expect an attack—but by a network of barbed wires, by which the hill and camp were fenced in. Quickly the wires were cut. That done, some of the burghers charged the tents, while the rest made for the enemy's trenches on top of the hill.

How awful a surprise! Taken unawares, the foe ran to their strongholds, but only to meet death there, for these were already in possession of our men. Myburgh, a Gastron burgher, so very brave, was the first and only one to receive a mortal wound—other men were slightly wounded in that hand-to-hand struggle. At dawn the hill and the camp were in our possession, for the enemy, after a loss of 9 killed and wounded, thought it best to resist no longer.

With the occupation of the hill it was possible to reach the village. The British allowed the burghers to pass their skanzes without shooting at them. But no sooner had they entered the village than a heavy fire from the forts was directed against them. They were not slow to respond to this reception, and that so effectively that the commanding officer was soon willing to entrust himself with his 130 men to our keeping. All was over.

At 3 P.M. we departed. The English commandant and his men accompanied us for some distance, and then we dismissed them after their having promised that they would remain strictly neutral.

CAPTAIN SPANDOW SURPRISED.

While operating in the Cradock district I learnt that a certain Captain Spandow, with about ninety men, was on the track of a small party of Boers. Only *ninety*! The small number tempted us to try to effect their capture, which, as a rule, was not a very difficult nor dangerous operation. Taking forty burghers I started at midnight, and at dawn found myself still six miles from the enemy. Lest they should escape I took twelve men with the best animals, and with these proceeded ahead, so as to engage the enemy until the rest, whose horses were very tired, should come to our assistance.

About half an hour after sunrise we unexpectedly lighted on the pickets of the enemy, who camped for the night in the Waterkloof valley, twenty miles from Cradock. The pickets were charged and captured, and we seized a position hardly 200 yards from the English, who had off-saddled at a wall.

A brisk firing from both sides then ensued. The wall served the enemy in good stead. From there they could fire volley after volley on us. But gradually we crept nearer, until at last a few of the burghers had passed the wall, and were now on the side of the enemy, so that the wall could afford them no cover. While the men were trying to get on the other side of the wall, one of my adjutants—Hugo, a lad of thirteen summers—was killed, and two others wounded. But the British, now exposed to a cross-fire, suffered heavily. Several of them dropped down, either dead or wounded.

When I saw how untenable their position was becoming I sent in a flag of truce, asking them to surrender, so as to avoid unnecessary bloodshed. One of the officers sent word that, seeing Captain Spandow had already fallen, and their losses were so great, he considered further resistance useless.

We found that 15, including the captain, were killed, and 14 wounded. Six of the wounded died soon after their surrender. One of their men was at once sent to Cradock for an ambulance. Our losses were 1 killed and 2 wounded.

The men I had left behind had off-saddled, and so only arrived after the enemy had surrendered. The officer, on inquiring where our men were, and who had engaged them, only shook his head when I told him that we were but 13, and that 3 of these had been put out of action almost at the beginning of the engagement. The British numbered 84 in all. We were again provided with a good supply of ammunition, and 105 horses in excellent condition.

Some months later Major Warn's column was attacked at the same place by Commandant L. Wessels. Several of the enemy's horses were shot down, while a number of men were wounded. So suddenly had they to turn back, that many a helmet dropped down and the owner had no inclination to pick it up. The English had fallen once more into an awkward trap from which they had to extricate themselves with the utmost speed.

On another occasion Commandant Fouche awaited the enemy at the same spot and made about 150 prisoners. Long

Kloof Valley has thus become a noted place. The traveller passing through that valley will always be reminded of the South African War on seeing the fourteen graves alongside the road, and near to the stone wall.

SPRAGGE'S COLUMN CAPTURED.

The following report, bearing on Colonel Spragge's surrender, has been submitted to me by my military secretary, R.D. McDonald.

> "On the 27th of May, 1900, Spragge entered Lindley. Our commando was then stationed at a farm eight miles to the north of the village. General Colvile, whom Spragge was to have joined here, left early on the morning of the 27th. What urged him on we could not guess. Had he waited another day, Spragge would not have been captured. We followed him up for some miles, and inflicted slight losses on his rear.
>
> "At noon the burghers returned to the laager. About an hour before sunset our scouts returned with the news that the English had reoccupied Lindley, and that it was but a small column *without* guns. When the burghers heard that the column was only 500 strong, and had no guns, they required no other inducements, but started immediately for Lindley. Our men are, as a rule, more daring if they discover that the enemy has no cannons at their disposal; the big, monstrous guns they do not like. We had thus decided that this detached column would receive every attention from us.
>
> "The British, being warned by the dust in the distance that our commando was coming, considered it wiser to quit the village, fall back on Valsch River and occupy positions on the right bank of it. Darkness had now set in,

and we could do no more than place our pickets round the column. We had, however, not enough men that night to make sure that should the enemy try to escape they would not succeed. Forsooth, we were greatly surprised to find them still there the following morning. It seemed to us a little over-bold on their part to stay on with only two Maxims at their command. We did not know then that it would take us three and a half days, and some precious lives, before the white flag would be hoisted. The next day we surrounded them completely and thus knew that unless reinforced they would have to surrender.

"Early in the morning firing commenced; but the enemy had occupied during the night such strong positions—the hills and ridges on the river banks—that they were quite secure. We had the bed of the river, from whence we could not inflict such losses as would compel the enemy to capitulate. They held the key of the positions, and unless we could seize that stronghold, all our efforts would be useless. The question was, how to take it. Without the assistance of guns it was a dangerous and risky undertaking to charge that particular position—a hill on the right bank of the river. Our men, in charging it, would be exposed to a rifle and Maxim fire for at least 800 yards. Under cover of guns, however, it was possible to reach the hill. A gun was immediately sent for, and on the evening of the third day of the siege it arrived at Lindley.

"That night the gun was placed in position, and at dawn the hill was shelled. I stood watching the shells, as one after the other exploded on the hill. Not a living object was visible, none stirred, and so still (I shall not say at ease) did the English lie in the skanzes that I remarked to Prinsloo: 'General, it seems the enemy has abandoned the hill during the night, else we must already have seen some signs of them.'"

"After we had bombarded the hill for some time, a number of burghers charged it. Breathlessly we stood watching these gallant chargers. Arrived at the foot of the hill, they dismounted, and began climbing it. For some time all went well, when lo! a fire was directed against them from the summit. Being quite coverless on the slopes of the hill, they were forced to retreat. As they retreated the enemy rose to their feet and fired as briskly as they could at them. When we saw the English on top of the hill we mistook them for Boers, and began to clap hands and cheer, thinking that the hill had been taken by our men. We were soon disillusioned.

"As the burghers retreated, something strange and inexplicable occurred, which really decided the fate of the enemy. It was this: the burghers had hardly gone 300 yards, when the British abandoned *en masse* the hill, and retreated, almost as fast as the former, in the opposite direction. Whether they feared another and more determined onslaught, or whether there was the usual misunderstanding, I wot not. Be it as it may, the position we so coveted was abandoned; it was for us to seize it at once. With a little encouragement the charge was repeated, the hill taken, and in less than twenty minutes the white flag announced the surrender of Spragge's column.

"Between 60 and 70 of the enemy were wounded and killed, while the rest were made prisoners. It was their first interview with the Boers. After a four days' siege a bath and a good meal must have been welcome.

"From the veldt we took our surrendered friends to the village. The wounded were placed in the local hospital, and the officers found lodgings for the night in an hotel.

"I escorted Spragge to the village. On the way he had a long talk with me about the war, and wished to know why the Free State had cast in her lot with the Transvaal. He failed to see, and had to be reminded that Free Staters and Transvaalers were essentially one people; that the Vaal River divides the two States, but not the people, as far as blood was concerned.

"On being asked why they had evacuated the hill, which was their chief stronghold, he replied: 'That was a mistake.' We do not object to such mistakes. If this had not been committed, Spragge would in all probability have remained a free man, and his column would not have fallen into our hands, for that was our last and only chance. Early the next morning the reinforcements appeared on the adjacent hills, but they were too late to rescue Spragge's column. The prisoners were sent on to Reitz, and from there to the Transvaal."

The three seated in the centre are MR. MCDONALD, COMMANDANT LOUIS WESSELS, and the late LIEUT. P. TROSKIE.]

CHAPTER IV

IN TIGHT CORNERS

Daring the event to the teeth ...
And danger serves among them.

—Shakespeare

Come, let us make an honourable retreat,
Though not with bag and baggage.

—Shakespeare

The above heading may seem strange, and yet we presume that most officers, as well as many privates, who had taken a leading part in the late South African War can record many instances where they escaped by the skin of the teeth.

How often a shell exploded like a thunder-clap in one's immediate vicinity! How many a bullet just missed its mark as by a hair's breadth, whizzing past the ear with lightning speed! Well I remember how, on one occasion, a shell exploded right overhead with such tremendous force that both rider and horse rolled in the dust by the violent concussion produced by the explosion. The burghers, some distance away, watching me, thought that would be the last of Kritzinger. To their surprise I rose again, shook off the dust, mounted my steed, and rode on to the position they were defending.

At present I shall not dwell on deliverances from the fire-spouting machines of modern warfare, but confine my remarks to such escapes as were connected with attempts on the part of the enemy, either to secure my person or capture my commando. Here again I shall only cite some instances; to relate all will be tedious to reader and writer alike.

In the beginning of July, 1901, just a few days after we had so successfully attacked and taken James Town, we arrived at a farm situated on the banks of the Kraai River, eighteen miles from Lady Grey. Here was the enemy's opportunity.

The owner of the farm—Van der Merwe, a most loyal colonist—was not at home, but, as we learnt afterwards, had gone to Lady Grey, or to the nearest English column, to announce the presence of my commando in his neighbourhood. Of this unfriendly deed we were altogether unaware.

As soon as we had off-saddled, our scouts were sent out in different directions. In the evening they returned with the report that for miles around us no traces of the enemy were to be seen. The pickets for the night were then put out on the three main roads leading to the farm, which was in a valley almost entirely encompassed by high and rugged mountains.

With my pickets out I felt at ease. I went to the farm-house, had dinner, got a room, and laid myself down to enjoy the night's rest, on which the enemy was soon to intrude so violently.

About 2 A.M. one of the pickets came to the laager to report a noise, which sounded like the tramp of horses, but he could not, on account of the intense darkness, see any objects. Warned by this report, we began to make preparations for an attack. Veldt Cornet Kruger was at once ordered to ascertain the truth of the report. But before he had left the camp one of the burghers came back and assured us that it was a herd of cattle.

Thus reassured, we betook ourselves to rest. Rest? No, certainly not. The foe is at hand. No sooner had we wrapped ourselves up in the blankets when, behold! rifle reports grated on our ears. The herd of cattle was nothing else than Colonel Scobell's column. Alas! our pickets had been cut off and hence could not report on the enemy.

Imagine our position! I began dressing as fast as I could, faster than ever before in my life. So near was the enemy, that when I reached the back door of the house in which I slept they had already entered by the front door. Had it not been for some plucky burghers the enemy would have completely cut off my exit and I would have been captured.

Fortunately the way was still open at the back door. What a scene I witnessed outside! Friend and foe were so intermingled, and engaged in hand-to-hand fight, that it was impossible to distinguish the one from the other. Right in front of the door the gallant Commandant Calmon Caechet was wrestling with an opponent that proved too strong for him. Next to him a certain Grobler had floored his man, and was handling him so roughly that the poor fellow called for help. The one who was too strong for Caechet left him to render assistance to his brother in adversity. Grobler then left his prey, and both he and Caechet seized their rifles and made for better regions.

Thinking that it might be only a patrol of the enemy that had come upon us incidentally and not intentionally, I tried hard to get the rather panic-stricken burghers into action. At a gate through which they had to pass I stopped them, and ordered them back. We soon noticed, however, how serious our position was; in fact, that we were surrounded on every side, and would have to fight our way through and out.

At about 3.30 A.M. the British brought their guns into action. The mountains resounded with the explosion of the shells, and the night was illuminated by the flashes of the guns. The fireworks were magnificent beyond description, but ... we had no inclination to admire them under such circumstances.

The next morning we counted our losses: ten burghers were captured, two wounded and one killed. One hundred and thirty horses were missing, most of the men were without saddles, and only a few had blankets.

This was indeed a surprise, and yet we were astonished that, after all, any of us did escape. So eager was the enemy to secure my person, that they did not attend to the burghers, whom they had disarmed, but simply flung their rifles aside and left them to themselves. The men, thus disarmed, instantly picked up their rifles and "trapt," *i.e.*, ran off. Thus very few of them were without rifles the following day.

Our feelings cannot be easily described. There were forty-six men who had to go on foot. A large number had no saddles. I lost all my horses. The only hope we entertained was that the British Government would soon restore our property. What we regretted most was the loss of our men.

Two of our pickets were caught, the remaining six, when charged and cut off, had taken refuge in a deep ditch, where they remained until the enemy had left, and then found their way back to the commando.

My next escape, though not exposed to the enemy's fire, and perhaps not even known to them, was probably the narrowest I had during the whole campaign.

We were again hard pressed by two columns. Our horses being very tired, we were obliged to rest them for a short while, even at the risk of falling into the hands of the enemy. Our way led through a valley, bordered on both sides by huge mountain ranges which for at least six miles ran parallel.

On the side of the road, half-way up the valley, was a farmstead where we off-saddled and gave our horses some fodder. The two columns which were on our track had been coming nearer. Fortunately darkness was setting in. When the front column was a short distance from us, we saddled and went to a dense bush close to the road. In that bush we delayed, till the first column had passed us and advanced some distance. As the second was only one or two miles behind the first, and as we were not sure whether it would also pass, we fell in behind the first; there was but one road.

We were now between two columns. We rode on as quietly as we could, hardly a whisper was heard. The slightest noise on our part could betray our presence. We were so close to the front column that we could distinctly hear the rumbling of wheels and the tramp of horses. Should the progress of the column be in any way obstructed, hereby causing a standstill, the one at our rear would inevitably press us upon the front one. What cold drops of perspiration rolled over my forehead! How I held my breath! Who shall describe the anxiety of such moments? There was but one way open—the way to the stars and the Throne beyond the stars. Before and behind us the foe, on both sides mountains, so steep and rugged that it would be folly even to attempt to climb them. Wistfully we looked up.

After riding some distance we met a native that belonged to the front column. He had tarried a little too long. We addressed him in English, and thus put him off the scent altogether. Mistaking us for English, he told us all he knew about the different columns. In this way we rode along, gradually approaching the extremity of the two ranges. Out at last! How relieved we felt can hardly be imagined. Once more we breathed freely. The poor native! How startled he was when he discovered his mistake, and learnt that he was then a prisoner, and had to accompany us.

On the 13th of October, 1901, the enemy had very ingeniously laid a trap for me, and had almost drawn me into it.

At that time we were in the district of Wepener, a village on the Basutoland border. Several British columns were then operating in that district. As so many were concentrated there, it was extremely hazardous and difficult for small commandoes, such as ours, to move during the daytime. The space between the Caledon River and Basutoland in which we could move becoming daily more and more circumscribed and limited, we determined to cross the Caledon River. Besides, we heard that the river was rising, and so were anxious to ford it before it was in flood.

On the evening of the 12th of October we set out in the direction of the river. At 10 P.M. we arrived at a farm, where we halted till 1 A.M. It was our intention to stop at this farm for the night, but owing to some strange foreboding of imminent danger I resolved to leave; and at 1 A.M. gave orders to saddle. As it was a very dark and cold night, some of the burghers felt reluctant to leave, and I heard them saying, "What is up again to-night with General Kritzinger?

Surely we are perfectly safe here! Why trek again in the bitter cold at midnight?" But my orders had to be obeyed, and at 2 A.M. we were on the march.

Five of the men, who could not find their horses in the dark, were left behind to seek them when it was light. At daybreak that farm was surrounded and shelled by the enemy. Had we remained there we would have been in a sad plight; the five men were all captured. We escaped, but there was another trap for the next day. We off-saddled at a farm three miles from the river. Commandant Wessels, three burghers and myself rode to the Drift—"Basters Drift"—to see whether the stream was still fordable.

Little dreaming that the enemy was concealed on the opposite bank of the river, behind the ruins of an old homestead, and was watching us as we gradually approached the river, we entered the stream and waded through it. Arrived on the opposite side we sent one of the men back to call the commando, for the river was rising rapidly. The other two burghers were sent to reconnoitre ahead, while Wessels and myself remained on the bank of the river.

Scarcely had the two men left us, when we were startled by rifle reports close by. We jumped up, ran to our horses, and saw that we were hardly 100 yards away from the enemy. All we could do was to recross the river, and that had to take place in a shower of bullets. Let one imagine himself in a swollen river, so deep that his horse has to swim now and then, and the foe on the bank directing an incessant fire on him, and he will realise to some extent our position. We reached the bank safely, but had to do another 800 yards to get out of harm's way.

The two men we had sent ahead—what became of them? Alas! they rode into the jaws of death, for when they discovered the enemy they were hardly 15 yards from them. "Hands up!" resounded from behind the wall. The men, rather than surrender and sacrifice their commando, made an ill-fated attempt at escape. In the twinkling of an eye they were shot down. The one—a young Trichard from Cradock—was dead on the spot; three bullets penetrated his body. The other—young Wessels from Winburg—was wounded in the leg and captured.

These two brave young men were the means of saving Wessels and myself either from being captured or shot. And not only that, but their gallant action, in which the one forfeited his life, and the other a limb, proved the salvation of the whole commando. If they had surrendered Wessels and I would probably have gone in the same direction, and the commando would have followed, and so all of us would have been in a terrible predicament. But they had risked their lives to save us from certain destruction.

Failing to ford the river at that drift, we proceeded downstream with the hope of crossing it somewhere else. To our disappointment the river had risen to such a degree that the only transit still left could be a bridge. Now there was but one far down the stream, and it was very doubtful whether that was not held by the enemy. Anyway, we were going to try, and so marching almost all the whole night we arrived at the bridge a little after sunrise. How glad we were to find the bridge still unoccupied! We had just reached it in time, for half an hour after we had gone over the British took possession of it. They had now completed their cordon; but we—were out of the circle.

On the 22nd of the same month we were once again in tight corners—surrounded by three columns.

As we found no rest either for ourselves or our animals in the south-eastern districts of the Orange Free State, we resolved to go to the Winburg and Ladybrand districts.

The enemy had pitched their camps all along the main road from Reddersburg to Dewetsdorp, and from there to Wepener. These stations were from six to eight miles apart, and formed a kind of fence. Through this line we had to pass, as well as the blockhouse line extending from Bloemfontein to Ladybrand, *via* Thaba 'Nchu.

We left at dusk, got safely through the camp-line, and rode on till 2 A.M., when we arrived at a certain farm. We went to the house to make inquiries as to the enemy. A woman opened the door, and on learning who we were, informed us that a quarter of an hour from her home an English column was encamped. How disgusting! We had been in the saddle from sunset to 2 A.M. and here we were, just a quarter of an hour from the enemy. We thought and hoped that we were then at least twelve miles from the nearest column. Why not engage them? the reader might ask. Well, we did. But our horses, which had to live on the tender grass-shoots, needed a rest very badly; we could hardly use them. Besides, there was a blockhouse-line to pass the following night, and this one was still 24 miles off.

We proceeded another three miles, to be at least four miles from that column. At about 2.30 we off-saddled. Being not quite at ease we rose after a short rest and re-saddled. Two scouts were sent to a hill close by. To their surprise they found the enemy's pickets stationed on the same kopje, at the foot of which the British camp was pitched. Having said "good-morning" to each other in military fashion the two returned with the unwelcome news that the enemy was just next door. We had slept side by side without knowing of each other. Ignorance was bliss that night.

This column—about 200 strong—on discerning us, at once prepared for action. Though very tired, we took up positions and began to engage the advancing foe. We succeeded in checking their progress, and certainly had the best of the situation till noon, when the scene was changed. My scouts returned with the alarming report that two other columns were advancing on us from Thaba 'Nchu.

I saw that we could not afford to lose a moment, for the two columns were not far apart, nor at any great distance from us. If we should continue the fight with the one the others would meet and we would be surrounded. Hence I gave instructions to the men to fall back. The report reached us unfortunately too late—our exit was already cut off. The enemy had occupied positions all around us, and there we were, right in the centre of a circle whose circumference consisted of an unbroken line of enemies. My secretary, who had never before been in such a circle, asked me: "Now, General, what now? What is our next move?" "We must charge that column in front of us," I replied, and, suiting the action to the word, we went off as fast as our tired horses could go, making straight for the enemy. This was too much for them; they first halted, and then—retreated to a ridge about 1700 yards to their left. This retreat afforded us an exit. We were, however, exposed to a cross-fire for fully three miles, but it proved ineffectual, for only one burgher was slightly wounded.

If the enemy had not retreated that day, or had only occupied a certain brook, through which we had to pass, it would have been impossible for us to escape. But if there were no *ifs* there would not have been such a lamentable war in South Africa. Neither would such unpardonable blunders have been committed.

We were glad that the enemy had allowed us to pass. That

night we crossed the fighting-line near to Sprinkhaan's Nek, where General De Wet and his men had such a hot reception.

BETWEEN TWO RIVERS AND FIVE COLUMNS.

On the evening of the 14th of March, 1901, my commando crossed the Tarka River, after which Tarka Stad is named. As heavy rains were falling we bivouacked not far from the river. There in the veldt, without any shelter, we spent a miserable night, for we were exposed to incessant showers, which drenched us to the very skin. But there was something even worse in store for us the following day.

Having crossed the Tarka River, we were between that river and another called Vlekpoort River, which flows into the Tarka some six miles from where we had forded the latter.

The following morning we rode to a farm near by. There we off-saddled, fed our horses, and began to prepare our breakfast. How stiff, cold and hungry we were! We could hardly wait until the meat was thoroughly broiled. Just as we began to satisfy the pangs of hunger the scouts came back, and once more it was "opzaal! opzaal!" (saddle! saddle!). We knew what it meant. The enemy was on our heels.

Two columns were on our right flank, between the two rivers. One had followed us up, and was then on the banks of the Tarka River; another was encamped in front of us on the banks of the Vlekpoort River; whilst a fifth was stationed near the confluence of the two streams. Thus five columns all around us; and the problem to be solved was, how to get out of the net.

This problem we solved in a practical manner. We occupied at once the strongest positions we could find, and, fortunately for us, between the rivers were natural positions so strong, that, with a small number of men, it was possible to hold one's own against great odds. These positions we seized, and were determined to stand or fall thereby. We would fight to the last cartridge, and then try and break through the cordon during the night.

In the meanwhile the enemy had drawn nearer. At about 8 A.M. the fighting commenced. From different directions shell after shell was hurled upon us. Again and again the enemy charged us, but was beaten back with greater loss to themselves than to us. Retreat? We could not. Surrender? That was out of the question; so from morn till sunset we clung to our positions, as though we were tied to them, and defended our persons as resolutely as possible.

Just as the sun was setting we stormed one of the enemy's positions. And although three of the burghers were wounded, the rest succeeded in expelling the enemy. Our way was now open; when darkness set in we could recross the Tarka. A pom-pom fire was opened upon us from the column on our left flank as we crossed the stream, which was then so high that our horses had to swim. Owing to the darkness none were injured.

The following day we had the pleasure of capturing the Commandant of Tarka Stad with his escort. The enemy was so sure of our surrender that a report was sent to Tarka Stad to the effect that we were quite surrounded, and that they hoped to deliver us the following morning at 8 o'clock. And as they might require some more ammunition to force us to surrender, the military must forward some.

The commandant of the village was taking this ammunition out when we met him. His men, riding in twos and threes at some distance apart, were disarmed by us without wasting bullets on them. At last the commandant, who happened to be some distance behind, came riding up to us. As he came on I rode up to him and said in a friendly tone: "Old chap, you'd better let me have your gun." Thinking that I was imposing upon him, he said: "Come along; don't play the fool!" When I had assured him that I was in earnest he remarked: "But surely you are not a Boer. Kritzinger's commando is the only one in the district, and that is surrounded." Then taking the report out of his pocket he said: "Just read this—'Kritzinger surrounded, will be captured and brought in to-morrow.'" Imagine his astonishment on learning that he was then addressing the very man whom he had hoped to meet as a prisoner-of-war.

He handed me his rifle. After that we had a long conversation, and enjoyed a drink together, as though we had never been at war.

The ammunition and horses were confiscated, and came in very useful after the engagement of the previous day. The commandant and his party were then dismissed.

AGAINST THE RAILWAY.

Towards the end of July, 1901, large forces of the enemy had concentrated upon my commando. Our only salvation then lay in crossing the Port Elizabeth railway line, near which we then were.

After a day's fighting we set out to the line, but to our great disappointment and embarrassment we found the line securely guarded by armoured trains, which made it impossible for us to cross during the day.

The enemy had followed us up, and there was no chance of retracing our steps. All we could do was to resist the foe till it was dark, and then try to escape. This we did, and succeeded in repelling the enemy. The burghers fought bravely, but at sunset they were forced to evacuate their positions and withdraw to a mountain next to the railway line.

This was our last position. We could go no farther. In front of us was the railway, behind and on our flanks the British columns. Indeed, an uncomfortable situation! We fought until it was quite dark; then the firing ceased, and we had time to plan an escape. And this is what we did. At 11 o'clock that evening numerous fires were kindled on the top of the mountain. We knew that these fires would be misleading; the enemy, as long as they saw the lights, would think that we were still on the mountain, and, being less watchful, we might slip through.

At 12 o'clock we saddled. We were going to try to pass through the enemy's line. On we rode, silently and guided by the sentinels' fires; we knew exactly which spots to avoid. Every moment brought us nearer to our doom or deliverance. Shall we succeed or not? we anxiously asked ourselves. Unnoticed we passed the foe and were free once more.

The next morning only the ashes of our fires were surrounded. As a shower of rain had fallen the same night, wiping out the footprints of our horses, the British certainly wondered what became of us. The Boers had again disappeared so mysteriously.

I shall conclude this chapter with two striking incidents. On the 13th of August, 1901, we came in conflict with the British forces in the district of Venterstad, Cape Colony. During the engagement I observed that the enemy was bent on a certain position which, if seized, would enable them to surround us. Now the Boer never likes to be surrounded. There is nothing that he dreads so much as a siege. To keep my way open, I took a number of burghers, and with these occupied the position referred to. Having stationed them there I rode back to the hill where I had been before. Unfortunately this hill had been deserted in the meanwhile, and was then held by the enemy.

Seeing a number of horses at the base of the hill I concluded that the burghers were still there and thus rode on without the slightest apprehension. Arrived at the foot of the hill, I looked up, and to my astonishment saw a large greyhound with the men. This made me suspicious. One of them at once called out: "Hands up! Come here, you beggar!" I was with the wrong party. Surrender? Verily not. I turned my horse, gave spurs, and off we went, horse and rider carried, as it were, by bullets which whistled past my head with deafening noise. For a considerable distance I was exposed to this shower of bullets. My horse received two wounds, but brought me out unscathed. That night I was cut off from the commando, and all the burghers thought that I was shot or captured. To their delight and surprise I joined them the next day again. That same day I was to have as marvellous an escape as the day before.

From early morn we were engaging the foe. While the fight was going on I took nine men to occupy a certain hill. This hill was already in the possession of the enemy, but we were not conscious of that, and thus unwittingly rode on to our doom.

The enemy had carefully hidden on the hill, and without challenging us opened a terrible fire upon us just as we arrived at the foot of the hill. Seeing that we were only a small party it certainly was not manly on their part to fire before challenging us. All the men but one were instantly wounded or killed, and their horses shot down. One of them escaped on foot. Strange—perhaps incredible to some—I came out with my horse and that uninjured.

At the close of the war I met the officer who was in command on that hill. He told me that as we came riding up to the hill he recognised me and told his men: "There, Kritzinger is coming; let us make sure of him." I happened to be riding a black horse, taken from one Captain King. That horse was so well known to the enemy that at a great distance they could recognise me.

These are some of the narrow corners in which we found ourselves during the war. I could multiply them, but 'tis needless. They will give the reader some idea of what we often had to pass through.

CHAPTER V

TO THE CAPE COLONY

From March to December, 1901, the area of war operations was limited exclusively to the two Republics. All the British forces were concentrated there. Gradually the fact dawned upon us that, unless we contrived to draw the British forces, in some way or other, off the Republics, the latter would eventually be exhausted of all provisions, which would necessitate their surrender. They could not for ever supply Boer commandoes and British columns with provisions, especially when farming pursuits were so disturbed and hampered by the enemy. It became quite clear that, in the event of a long campaign, our whole salvation would be in the Cape Colony. There we would be drawing on the enemy's resources, and the British Government would indirectly be supporting us in compensating colonists for losses sustained by Boer commandoes. An additional advantage, should the scene of operations be transferred from the Republics to the Cape Colony, would be that many colonists would enlist in our ranks. There we should be constantly recruited, and our commandoes would increase rather than decrease. That was an advantage not to be despised, for our forces were getting daily weaker in the states.

With such facts before him, General De Wet planned a second invasion of the Cape Colony towards the close of the year 1901. By the end of November we met him with his forces, about 1500 strong, in the district of Bethulie. After a few days' fighting with the forces of General Knox on the farms Goede Hoop and Willoughby, we left for the Orange River, which we intended to ford at Odendaal's Stroom, a drift fifteen miles below Aliwal North.

As heavy rains began to fall, we were anxious to reach the river before it was in flood. Day and night through rain and mud we ploughed on towards the river. When we reached the Caledon River we saw that the water was rising rapidly, and began to fear that the Orange River, which was still thirty miles off, would be impassable. Well, we were going to try. We increased our speed, and left behind scores of tired horses and mules.

The 1st of December, at sunset, we arrived on the banks of the river. But what a disappointment! A rolling mass of water before us, so deep and strong that there was no chance to pass through. And there we were between two rivers in flood, with a narrow strip of country between them, and thousands of the enemy on our track. We knew that the English could seize the bridges, of which there are but a few, and could then be reinforced from all parts of the country to hem us in so closely that escape would be impossible. De Wet would at last be "cornered" and forced to surrender—so, at least, the enemy thought. Our situation seemed, nay was indeed, very critical.

To delay and wait for the fall of the river was out of the question. For not only would it take at least fifteen days before the river would have subsided to such a degree that we could hope to ford it, but De Wet's old friend, General Knox, was at his heels. All we could do was to march up the

Caledon. That river, being much smaller than the Orange River, would sooner fall and afford us a way of escape. Our hopes were realised. De Wet found a ford where he and his whole commando passed through. Once more he was a free man. We accompanied him for some distance up the river, until we came to the farm of one Smith. Here Captain Scheepers, Captain Fouche and myself left the main body and went with our commando, consisting of about 300 men in all, in the direction of Rouxville, where, on the 13th of December, we captured 150 of the 2nd Brabants, who were sent to and *for* us.

While in the Rouxville district we received a message from De Wet that we should enter the Colony as soon as possible, and that he would try to follow us up. He was, however, prevented from carrying out his intentions. It seemed as if Providence had so ordained it that he should not cross the Orange River, or, even crossing it, should not sojourn for a long time in the land of the enemy. For no sooner had he passed the Caledon, than the enemy concentrated on him and succeeded in driving him back through Sprinkhaan Nek to the northern districts of the Orange Free State.

This, however, afforded us a chance of slipping through on to British soil. In the night of the 15th of December, at 2 A.M., we forded the Orange River at a point five miles below Odendaal's Stroom. It was a dark night, and the water was still very high, but we all reached the opposite bank in safety. There we came upon the guard of the drift, as they were indulging in a game of cards. One was wounded, two ran away and eight were captured. They did not expect us to cross the river at 2 A.M., and were thus taken unawares.

We were now once more in British territory. But what a contrast between this and our first invasion in the beginning of the war! No large commandoes, no waggons, and no guns.

We were only 300 men—a raiding band, as some contemptuously called us—with one Maxim, and even that proved too cumbersome, for we soon cast it into a pool. Instead of waggons and tents we had only our horses and mackintoshes, and some were even without the latter. No large supplies of ammunition; our bandoliers were almost all half empty.

The morning of the 16th of December, then, found us in the Cape Colony. We had made up our minds to spend at least some months in the enemy's country. Come what may, we would not return to the Orange Free State. If the British had the right to stay in the Republics, why should we not tarry awhile in the Colony? From the river we made a forced march to Venterstad, a small village lower down the stream. We needed an outfitting, and thought that that would be the most likely place where we would get it. We only had to surprise the garrison, about 50 strong, and we would have all we wanted. In this we were quite successful. The garrison, or town-guard, soon hoisted the white flag.

We could now fill our bandoliers, and requisition the necessary articles in clothing, boots, etc. But the enemy was not slow to follow us. We were just allowed sufficient time to take all we required, and then the columns came to remind us that we were strangers and intruders.

As we have related our experiences in other chapters, we shall not here enter into details. For at least seven months, after we had crossed the river, the enemy continually harassed us. We hardly enjoyed a single day's rest. During the day we had to fight, and during the night we had to trek. One thing was plain: the enemy was determined to silence us completely. That they did not succeed is almost passing strange. If 300 Britishers were to have entered the two republics, would they have proceeded very far?

General Hertzog had, at the same time, invaded the western province of the Cape Colony, but, being far away from the railway line, the British did not worry him very much. They all seemed to conspire against my small band, and had the additional advantage of railways on every side of us. Deeper and deeper into the heart of the Colony we were driven. We marched in a southern direction. Whither? We did not know, only forward. And so far did we push on that at length the vast expanse of the Indian Ocean loomed in the distance, and reminded us that it was time to retrace our steps, for we could certainly go no farther on horseback. So we slipped through the pursuing columns, and returned to the districts of Jansenville, Graaff-Reinet and Cradock.

In February we were not so hotly pursued. De Wet had entered the Cape Colony from the north-west; and like a magnet he drew most of the British forces irresistibly to him. This gave us a short rest, which was, alas! only too short. For De Wet, as well as Hertzog, had to fall back on the Orange Free State, and with redoubled energy the British came upon us like a mighty avalanche. The reader can hardly realise what we had to undergo these first eight months in the Cape Colony.

It was a bitter disappointment to learn how De Wet had fared and that both he and Hertzog had abandoned the Cape Colony. We knew it was not their fault and so did not blame them. Still we were resolved to hold out as long as possible. Gradually it went better; the colonists began to enlist and our numbers swelled. We could now form other commandos, and despatch these in various directions, and that prevented the enemy from concentrating all their forces on us. At last we had gained such a strong footing in the Colony that to expel us all was simply an impossibility.

And how did General De Wet fare when he crossed the

Orange River on the 11th of February, 1901? The following account given by one who accompanied him will give the reader some idea of the unsuccessful attempt at invasion.

"MY DEAR K.,—We are just back from the Cape Colony, and no doubt you will be anxious to hear all about our recent experiences. I daresay you have followed us all the while in thought, and have carefully studied the papers to ascertain our movements and learn what we were doing. As we have little faith in newspaper war-reports, I shall take the trouble to give you a full account of our short-lived colonial invasion.

"You will be surprised, and perhaps sorely disappointed, to hear that De Wet's and Hertzog's commandoes are all back in the Orange Free State. This means that you are going to have now ever so much harder times, for the enemy will certainly concentrate their forces on your small commando, to clear you out of the Cape Colony as soon as possible. The odds, of course, will be so great to contend against, that, humanly speaking, you will be bound to retreat across the Orange River. Still I trust that you will not follow our example, but will find the Colony quite large enough to baffle the enemy in their attempts to capture you. And as the British have already exerted themselves in vain for over three months to oust you, we entertain the hope that you will maintain your ground till reinforced.

"On the 11th of February we, *i.e.*, General P. Fourie's division, crossed the Orange River at Zanddrift, west of Philippolis. De Wet had taken possession of the drift the previous day, so our way was open, and as the river was low it was not difficult to ford it. With the exception of a few mules we sustained no losses. It was somewhat like a picnic, the burghers were as gay as could be. Being a very hot day they spent most of the time in the water. The guns and some other vehicles were dragged through the river by teams composed of sprightly young men. It was a sight to see 70 or 80 men before a gun or waggon in the stream. I could not help thinking in what a plight these would be should the enemy suddenly appear on the banks of the river. That, indeed, would be a surprise worth beholding. At sunset we were all on British soil.

"After the burghers had taken supper the whistle was blown and the oft-repeated command, 'opzaal,' sounded in their ears. That night we did not make a long trek, for both horses and men felt equally tired after the day's exertions. Still we had to cover at least eight miles, for it was not quite safe so near to the river. There were columns behind and columns in front of us, and columns on every side. After a wearisome march over a rugged and uneven road, if road it could be called, with intense darkness enveloping us, we finally reached the halting-place.

"The following morning at sunrise we started for Bezuidenhoud's farm, which was close by. There the burghers received their instructions from De Wet. With regard to their conduct in the Cape Colony it was pointed out to them that they should treat the colonists in such a way as would ensure their friendship. On no account were they to molest the peaceful neutral British subjects, for they were not at war with the colonists. They were also forbidden to take anything from British subjects without paying the proper value for the thing required. There were some more injunctions, which have escaped my memory. No wonder that one should forget when chased as we were. I believe these orders were, as a rule, obeyed. In fact I should say we erred in adhering so strictly to them, for we met some ultra-loyalists who would not give or sell us so much as a morsel of food. Now when any one is hungry, and people will neither give nor sell, what else can he do than help himself? If he does not, it is his own fault should he starve. At a certain farm we offered a sovereign for one bucket of meal, but all in vain; when we asked the woman for a glass of water, she pointed us to a spring some distance off. Shameful, is it not! Next time we shall, I am afraid, not be so over-polite. One learns a lot every day.

"At 11 A.M. our scouts reported that they had sighted two columns about 7 miles from us. And now our troubles and hardships commenced. What we anticipated and dreaded had actually taken place. The enemy had occupied all the passes in front of us, preventing us thereby from crossing the railway at the intended point between Norval's Pont and Colesberg. We had now to go in that barren and desolate part of the Colony where one is entirely dependent upon forage, and where, unfortunately for us, none was to be had.

"I expected that the British would intercept us. They knew about De Wet's intended invasion; and had every facility by rail for mobilising and seizing all the points of consequence. Whilst we had to ride all the way from Winburg district, they had the advantage of being transported by rail—an advantage which can hardly be over-estimated.

"Encumbered with guns and waggons, we could not dodge the enemy. We either had to seize the passes or proceed in a direction which might lead to fatal results. To do the former appeared impossible to De Wet, and so the latter course was reluctantly adopted. If it were not for the convoy, we would have achieved our object and would have entered those districts where commandoes could exist.

"The enemy was engaged till dusk. We had no casualties; but Commandant Ross and a number of his men were cut off. They managed to reach the Orange Free State safely. How they found their way through the various columns, I can't say—a Boer, if need be, can retire wonderfully well! At sunset our convoy almost fell into the hands of the enemy. What a pity it did not! It would have saved us so much needless trouble, and we would have been far better off without it.

"Most of the night we remained in the saddle. The General was anxious to get as far away as possible from the columns, to rest his horses for a few hours. But the British, so it seemed, were resolved that neither we nor our horses should have a rest, for early the next morning they were on our heels. We could not offer any resistance, because we had no positions, and could not recklessly expose ourselves to the enemy's fire without any cover at all. On the open plain our horses would have been swept away by the enemy's guns, and in a short time we would have been all infantry. Hence, on their approach we withdrew, hoping to find a place where we could make a stand. Unfortunately we failed to find the wished-for positions. For miles and miles the country is just one vast plain; when you get to the end of that plain you may find a ridge, a hill or slight elevation, which, however, did not signify much. The enemy could easily outflank and surround us, if we did not abandon it in time. With eyelids "heavy and dim," and bodies "weary and worn," exposed to the dazzling rays of a burning sun, we rode on, driven occasionally as a herd of cattle. At last night fell and we could enjoy a short rest.

"The next morning the same story was repeated: the English hot on our track—no rest for body or soul. The country being as flat as the part we had traversed the previous day, we had to march again the whole day under a burning sun. Now and then we dismounted for a few minutes, in order that our horses might snatch a few mouthfuls of grass.

"At the hour of sunset there was something to relieve the monotony of fleeing all day. Two burghers—bread spies as we call them—had gone ahead to buy some bread at a farm where a party of the enemy was stationed. Not aware of that, they rode up to the house, with the result that one got captured, while the other returned under a hail of bullets at a breakneck pace to relate the fate of his comrade. De Wet immediately sent in a note asking the enemy to surrender, since they numbered only about twenty. They answered shortly: 'We won't.' They were then charged, and up went the white flag without their firing a single shot.

"For the night we bivouacked at that farm. The British columns were now scarcely four miles from us. We dreaded a night attack, but, owing to incessant rain, both parties seemed only too glad to stay where they were. Here we had the advantage of hills and ridges, where we could stand and face the foe.

"At sunrise the enemy's guns and Maxim-Nordenveldt began to play on these ridges. Our guns had been placed in position, too, and responded sharply. We succeeded in beating off the enemy's attacks till 11 A.M., then we were outflanked and had to evacuate our positions. Their losses must have been great. Two of our men fell in the action.

"From there we marched in the direction of the railway line, which we intended to cross that night near Houtkraal station. We were about seven miles from the line, and were very anxious to pass over. We were afraid that the

English would send on their forces by rail to guard the line and march upon us from in front, which, if done, could result in our complete annihilation. Besides, we intended, as soon as we were on the other side of the line, to divide our force into several commandoes and let these take different courses so that the enemy would not be able to concentrate any longer all their men on us. Thus wearily we dragged on through mud and rain to the line.

"To prevent armoured trains from cutting off our transit, men were sent ahead to destroy the line at two points. Here again we committed a few blunders for which we had to suffer. In the first instance the line was blown up at too early an hour that night, long before we were ready to pass over. The explosions reported our presence, and the armoured trains were despatched to restore the line. Then again, owing to the darkness the points where the line was destroyed were not sufficiently far apart. This we discovered when the enemy's guns began to roar and their shells exploded in our midst.

"Before reaching the line there was something to get through—a swamp at least 1500 paces broad. One can hardly have an idea what this swamp was like, and how much trouble it cost us and our poor animals to get through it. This was a veritable 'Slough of Despond.' It was covered with water from one side to the other, and we had to wade through knee deep, and sometimes the water reached to our loins. The water was no serious obstacle, but the ground was of a morass-like nature that our animals sank in to their knees and often to their girths. Most of the burghers had to dismount and lead their horses. Every now and then a horse would stumble, and down came the rider splashing in the mud and water. I led my faithful 'Klein Booi' all the way, walking knee deep through mud and water. Just think how we must have looked the following morning, with clogs of mud attached to our clothes, hands and faces, while our horses were baptised in mud! The waggons and guns gave us most trouble. It was quite impossible to get these through the swamp. They stuck in the mud, with draft animals and all. We had as many as fifty oxen before one waggon, but they could not move it an inch. Some mules sank in so deep that they could not extricate themselves, and were left to die in the mud!

"At daybreak the guns, De Wet's waggonette and a few carts were through the swamp; the rest of the convoy was still in it. General Fourie and a hundred burghers were left with the waggons while the commando proceeded to the line. At sunrise we were safely on the other side of the line, where we waited for Fourie. Suddenly, and very unexpectedly, a shell exploded in our midst, like a thunderbolt from a clear sky. I looked about to see whence it came; but before my eyes detected the armoured trains, another and yet another shell dropped in our midst. I say *in our midst*, for we were riding in close formation when these horrible projectiles were hurled upon us. As our horses were very tired and the veldt soaked through and through by the heavy rains, we could not scatter, nor ride fast, as we usually do when exposed to cannon fire in the open veldt. Thus slowly we rode on under this cannonade. And how wonderful none were injured! The hand of the invisible omnipresent God must have shielded us. At last we were out of the cannon's reach. Meanwhile the line had been repaired, the armoured trains moved freely up and down. Fourie, five other officers, and about a hundred burghers were now cut off from the commando. The burghers found their way back to the Free State; the officers followed us up, but, alas! met us only when we were on the point of recrossing the Orange River.

"In what a sorry plight we now were! Some of our ablest officers severed from us at a time when they were most needed. Their absence caused the greatest confusion, for now there were numbers of men without any officers. Besides, it was then impossible to carry out the idea of splitting up the commando without officers. Hence we were to be driven along by the overwhelming numbers at our rear. How many there were is hard to tell, but we caught up some of their despatches, from which we learnt that there were no fewer than fourteen columns in pursuit of us.

"Gradually we drifted into the most deplorable and wretched conditions. Our animals, owing to lack of fodder, began to give in. Scores of these we had to leave behind, some of them in excellent condition, but so starved that they could proceed no farther. The result was that hundreds of burghers had to walk, and they suffered most. How I felt for these unfortunates! They walked and walked until, exhausted and footsore, many a one dropped down along the road-side. There were those whose clothes were torn to fragments by the brambles through which they forced their way. They presented an appearance which evoked one's compassion.

"These men had to confront another enemy—hunger. They scarcely found time to prepare a meal, for when they arrived at the halting-place the first word they heard was, as a rule, "opzaal!" Thus footsore, battered, and with empty stomachs, these fellows had to march for miles and miles to escape the enemy's grip.

"I admired their power of endurance, patience, and determination. But admiration was not enough. I parted with all my horses, giving them to men who could walk no longer, and so walked on myself, until, footsore and exhausted, I too could go no farther. It was a pleasure to minister in this way to men who loved their country.

"If it were not for this determination on the part of De Wet's forces to keep out of the hands of the enemy, hundreds would have been captured, yet I believe not more than 250 prisoners were taken. As we went on our numbers gradually diminished. Those who were unable to keep pace with the main body broke off in small parties and found their way back to the Orange Free State.

"By the 19th we had pushed on as far as Brak River, about twelve miles from Prieska. Here we met with another disappointment, which almost proved fatal to our whole commando. The river was in flood and no transit possible. In what a dreadful plight we were! Hardly eight miles behind us the British columns were stationed in crescent shape; in front was the swollen Brak River, and nine miles to our right was the Orange River, and that in flood. Here at least it seemed as if De Wet would be caught, and though he escaped, this certainly was one of the tightest corners in which he ever found himself.

"About two hours before sunset we heard that the enemy was rapidly approaching us. Anxiously we asked ourselves, Whither now? We could not return, we could not ford the river; to proceed up-stream would expose us to the risk of being quartered against the river. There was but one course to follow, and that an extremely hazardous one. We could march down the Brak River as far as the Orange River, and then proceed along the latter. Between us and the enemy there was then a ridge, extending parallel with the Orange River. Behind this ridge we would be out of the enemy's view. Should they reach this elevation before it was dark, we would be pressed, with fatal consequences to ourselves, against a swollen river.

But here darkness proved our salvation once more. We proceeded down the Brak River and up the Orange River. When the enemy came to the ridge mentioned it was so dark that they could see no traces of us.

"De Wet had now decided to fall back on the Orange Free State. To many of us this was a bitter disappointment; but we saw that nothing else could be done under the circumstances. With tired horses and many burghers on foot we could not hope to circumvent the enemy. Others, especially those who had suffered most in walking, were enraptured at the idea of going back to the Free State. Their drooping spirits revived, and with renewed courage they started on the homeward march.

"The whole of that night we trekked along the banks of the Orange River, parallel to the British columns. We tried one ford after the other, but to our dismay the stream was impassable. The following day we were not only behind the enemy, but had outstripped them by nine miles. To gain more on them we kept up the march almost unbroken the whole day. And what a day it was! We had to walk from twelve to fifteen miles without a drop of water. Once we came to a forsaken well. The water was of a greenish hue, bitter and stagnant—a real Marah—but we drank to quench our thirst and moisten our parched lips.

"On the 22nd we had proceeded to a point six miles beyond the confluence of the Vaal and Orange Rivers. Here we found a small boat, and began at once to transport the dismounts. We knew that these, once across the river, would be in a safer position. Day and night we were engaged in taking these over; but the work progressed very slowly, for the boat could only take ten or twelve men at a time, and, besides, was so leaky that two had constantly to throw out the water. After 250 men had been ferried across the stream the approach of the enemy was announced, and so near were they that some of us had to depart in an almost half-naked state. About 80 burghers had to hide in the river until the storm was over. Almost all the vehicles were left behind while the main force retreated up the river.

"Fortune favoured me; I was among the lucky ones who found a seat in the boat as she was returning for the last time. Willie Louw and myself were appointed to supervise the boat, less the transport of the men be retarded in some way or other. For some time we worked together, and then Willie left me to manage alone. Though I was anxious to cross myself, I could not then leave the boat. When the report of the enemy reached us the burghers, eager to get through, stormed the boat from all directions. They forgot that if all want to get into the boat nobody will get across the river. What must be done? As there was no time for much deliberation I jumped in and expostulated with an excited crowd. None heeded, each pressed forward to get a place in the boat. I was finally compelled to threaten them with my revolver, but all in vain. No one was afraid. I believe they knew too well that I would not pull the trigger. One looked me straight in the face as I pointed the instrument to him and said, 'My dear fellow, you may shoot if you wish—I am not afraid; but I want to get through.' He completely disarmed me. I had no more threats.

"With an overcrowded boat we were at last on the stream, and finally reached the opposite bank, just as the enemy was beginning to shell De Wet's forces on the other side. It was indeed a relief to me, but we had to march another fifteen miles without water, exposed to scorching heat. At length we found some muddy water. Lying next to our horses we sipped up water so thick and muddy that we could hardly swallow it.

"As to De Wet's further movements I can hardly give you full particulars. He was followed up by the enemy, and had to abandon his guns the following day. Trying one drift after the other he succeeded at last in fording the river between Norval's Pont and Zanddrift; and so after seventeen days he was back in the Free State.

"Here you have a sketch of our attempt to invade British dominions. I have omitted many things of less interest. I wonder what you will think of all this. Looking back upon our adventures, it is, of course, easy to point out all the errors and blunders we have committed. We should, for instance, never have encumbered ourselves with a convoy and guns, which hampered our movements and were of very little service to us. Then again, we should not have crossed the river in one commando, but should have divided the force into at least twelve or fifteen commandoes, and these should have entered the Colony at different points, all moving in different directions, then the enemy could not have concentrated their hosts on us as they did. Besides, our discipline and organisation was poor, and it is a well-known fact that a thousand in disorder can accomplish less than two hundred well-organised men. But it is useless to dwell on these points. 'Tis easier to criticize the past than to forecast the future. Experience costs a great deal.

"Has our attempt been a complete failure? In many respects I should say it has. We have succeeded, however, in drawing the enemy out of the Free State, which was our chief object. And, though it did not cost them many lives, yet their following us in such desolate regions must have proved very expensive, and must have been a source of great hardship to themselves. If that be a consolation to know that we have not suffered alone, we have, then, at least one comfort.

"Brak River was the last nail in our coffin. If we only could have forded that, we would not have been ousted. On the other side of the river we would have found not only grass for our tired horses, but would also have been able to find remounts. Hertzog's commando was not far off, and they were strongly mounted, and could have rendered us great assistance.

"The president, who accompanied us, remained cheerful to the last, and, just as a common burgher, partook in all our troubles. Such a man we may well be proud of, and, I need hardly say, that we love and honour him all the more.

"As to the conduct of the burghers we need only remark that it was beyond praise. One never heard them grumble or murmur either against De Wet or any other officer. No rebellious complaints or threats were flung at the heads of those in authority. This, indeed, is typical of the Boer. He endures suffering and hardship with a submissive spirit and with a dignity which is remarkable. We do not marvel at this, for are they not formed of that stuff of which martyrs have been made in bygone years? And does not the blood of the French Huguenot course through the veins of many a one, while others are animated by the dauntless spirit of that little nation that combated the once mighty Spain for eighty years, and so achieved that honour and distinction which has secured for them an abiding place in the history of nations? Such men, who are willing to suffer and sacrifice all for freedom's sake, surely deserve to succeed at last.—Yours fondly,

"R.D. MCDONALD."

CHAPTER VI

WOUNDED

During the first days of August, 1901, the enemy seemed more determined than ever to effect my capture, or sweep me out of the Cape Colony, Very large forces concentrated on my commando, and pressed us so hard that our only safety lay in retreating to the Orange Free State. So hot was the pursuit that for forty-eight hours our horses were not once off-saddled.

On the 14th we arrived on the banks of the Orange River, near to Venterstad. We found the drift guarded by a small garrison of Hottentots that offered slight resistance. After a short skirmish they surrendered, and we waded safely through the stream. We were again on Free State soil, in our native land, where we knew almost every inch of the country.

Fording the river brought us no immediate relief; it rather increased our dangers. For we were now between two railway lines, each strongly guarded by blockhouses, while the space between the two lines was so confined and limited, that (with columns at our rear) we could not venture to delay there a day or two. So we had to cross one of these lines the same night. We decided upon the Springfontein-Bethulie line and thither directed our steps.

At about 8 A.M. we came in sight of the line, at a point six miles from Springfontein Junction. The sun had already risen. It was a bright morning, but our prospects were dark and ominous. We were confronted by a line studded with blockhouses and fenced in on both sides, while two armoured trains were belching forth clouds of steam and smoke in the distance. Behind us, and not far to our rear, the British columns were drawing nearer. We could but choose between two alternatives—surrender, or cut the wire at any cost. The former we could hardly give a thought; the latter must be done, and was successfully executed.

Our first attempt failed. The burghers, who had no cover, retreated when fire was opened upon them from the blockhouses. We fell back to a small hill not far from the line, and there we made up our minds that we *shall* cross. Commandant Louis Wessels—certainly one of the most intrepid and fearless officers of the whole Boer Army—made direct for the two railway gates, near which a blockhouse had been erected. These gates he opened, so that the burghers could proceed without any obstruction. Then in the face of blockhouses on every side, guards and armoured trains, we passed over the line. We were exposed to a shower of bullets, and to a terrific pom-pom fire, from the armoured train, but, to our amazement, without any effect. But for a few horses shot down, we would have achieved our object without any losses. The men marvelled and said Providence had protected them; the enemy probably attributed it to ill-luck and bad shooting. Both may be correct.

While passing over the line one of the men, accidentally or out of fright, had dropped and left his gun behind. He was ordered back, and had to pick it up under a storm of bullets. We could not afford to leave rifles behind. This was my first experience in crossing the British lines in daytime. Some time later I was to have a similar experience, which, as far as my person was concerned, proved less successful, indeed, almost fatal.

In regard to the blockhouse system, we need only make these general remarks. The blockhouses along the railway and fighting lines of the British, as well as in and round garrisoned places, played a most prominent part in bringing the war to an end. It was at all times difficult and dangerous to attack them; and to force their occupants to surrender involved greater loss of life on our part than we could prudently face. The only way we could destroy them was to approach them as near as possible during the night, and locate a dynamite bomb on or near them. In this way some of them have been blown up. It seems a barbarous process, but is not war, at its very best, barbarous, brutal, and unbefitting civilized nations?

As a means of capturing the burghers, they were a failure. Our commandoes, when driven against them, always had sufficient pluck and courage to cut the wires between them, and so they crossed the lines at almost any point they pleased. That we *have* crossed and recrossed them frequently is proof enough that they were, in this respect, not a success. The barbed wire fences, however complicated, were easily cut.

As a means of capturing the women and children, and especially the cattle, sheep and horses, they served the purpose well. It was almost impossible to drive a flock of sheep or a herd of cattle, not to mention horses, over these lines during the day. The women with the old and aged would retreat with the cattle and sheep until they came in touch with the blockhouses, and were then often captured, one and all.

If it had not been for these little shanties all over the two republics, it would have taken the British forces double if not treble the time to have so thoroughly exhausted the late republics of food supplies. When the republics were cut up into so many small sections it became impossible to protect our foodstuffs.

From the railway line we went to Rouxville district, where we enjoyed a rest of ten days. But on the 1st of September the enemy came in large numbers and till the 22nd of October harassed us almost daily.

As I was anxious to return to the commandoes I left behind in the Cape Colony, I thought it feasible to cross the fighting line, and take my commando to Ladybrand district, where the enemy would probably leave us unmolested for a while, and where the veldt provided ample food for our horses. Thither we directed our steps, and for a month we saw no signs of the British.

On the 23rd of November we were again south of the Bloemfontein-Ladybrand fighting line, and on our way to the Cape Colony. My first intention was to ford the Orange River near Aliwal North, but I soon realised that we would be incurring too great a risk in trying to cross the river there, for about twenty or twenty-five columns were then sweeping the southern districts of the Orange Free State. Now if the river was in flood these columns could press us against it, and we would then be in an awful predicament. So I resolved to cut the wire of the main line near Springfontein Junction, and from there march in the direction of Zanddrift, west of Philippolis.

Before that could be accomplished we had to beat our track through the columns already mentioned. And what a hearty reception they gave us! In one day we had to pass no fewer than eleven of these. And they *did* lift us up—so much so that we scarcely lighted on the ground. Even now I wonder how we contrived to escape these columns. We were fortunately provided with a number of picked horses, to which we must largely ascribe our salvation.

In what a dreadful state we found the country east of the lines! It resembled more a howling wilderness, a haunt of wild beasts, than an habitation of human beings. It was cleared of all stock; no living thing, and not a single burgher of other commandoes came in view. So thoroughly was the country cleared of all necessaries of life, that for six days we had to subsist on corn, coffee, and honey found in the mountains, for the bee-hives at the farms were all destroyed. On the 7th day, having cut the wire near Springfontein, we found large numbers of springbucks in Fauresmith district, and though our supply of ammunition was very limited, we could still afford to spare as many cartridges as would provide sufficient food for men reduced to starvation's point.

On the 15th of December we arrived at the river, and were ready to intrude once more upon British territory. During the day the river was carefully reconnoitred, so as to ascertain the best place to ford it. At nightfall we headed for it, and at 9 P.M. the commando was on its banks. In deep silence lest the guards woke up on the other side, and shielded by the wings of darkness, we began to ford the stream. Heavy rains had fallen higher up the river, in consequence of which the stream was so swollen that our horses had to swim about 150 yards. The men who could not swim had to rely exclusively on their horses, and clung to these for all life was worth. It was a very dark night, and as we only spoke in whispers, we succeeded in crossing the river, unobserved by the sentinels or guards, purposely stationed there to prevent our entering the Cape Colony. We were wet to the skin, six of the men were without clothes, some lost their horses, and others their rifles and bandoliers, but none their lives. We were indeed glad that we had attained our object. But we did not know what was in store for us.

At dawn we left the river, and moving southwards we soon encountered the enemy not far from the river. From early in the morning till late in the afternoon we were engaged by the enemy. At sunset we could off-saddle and rest our tired horses for a short while, and a hasty meal was prepared.

At dusk we mounted again, and rode till 11.30 that evening, to get some fodder. We arrived at a farm at midnight, but unfortunately it was already occupied by the enemy. We had no sooner fastened our horses and were lying down to rest, when the enemy began firing at us. We resaddled at once, and left the farm as quickly and quietly as possible. One of the burghers was wounded in the arm, the rest came out unhurt.

We now went in search of another farm, for it was a necessity that our horses should get some fodder. The night was very dark, and, being unacquainted with that part of the country, we began wandering, and we *did* wander until the guide and most of the men were asleep on their horses—wandered till we had described a circle and found ourselves, after a three hours' ride, almost at the very farm we had left that night. If it had not been for the flickering lights of the enemy's camp-fires, we should not have known where we were, and certainly would have been quite close to them the next morning. When we saw these lights, hardly three miles away, *then* we woke up.

I then took the lead, and brought the commando to the farm we were in search of.

At sunrise we arrived there, off-saddled, and gave our horses fodder. The pickets were put out, and breakfast was prepared. But, alas! before we could eat, the enemy was upon us, and our intended feast was converted into a prolonged fast. So near was the foe, and so rapidly did they advance, that we had scarcely time to saddle and seize the nearest ridges. If it had not been for the marvellous celerity of the Boer, many of the men would have been captured at that farm.

This was the 16th of December, 1901. The day I never shall forget in my life's history, and in the history of the Anglo-Boer War. The sun rose in splendour that morning, casting his rays upon me—a man in the prime of life, full of energy and martial ambition. At eventide the scene was changed! Weary, wounded and bleeding on a lonely plain, shrouded in darkness, I lay, no more the man of the day, or of bygone days, but weak and helpless as a babe.

Though I had taken part in many hot engagements, both as burgher and commander, and had been in many tight corners, yet I do not recollect a day in which we were so brought to bay, when we were so hard pressed as that day. Early in the morning it was evident that the enemy had but one design that day, and that was to force me to surrender. My commando was about eighty strong. On my flanks were continually two British columns, whilst a third one was following up at my rear. With such a small number of men at my disposal, and three columns to oppose, it was next to impossible to offer successful resistance. We had hardly taken up a position when the flanking columns would come round, and we had either to abandon the position or allow ourselves to be shut in. Thus we were compelled to retreat from one to another position, under the rays of a December sun, which seemed to set everything on fire, through a country so parched and dry that one hardly found a drop of water to quench one's thirst, and that from early morn till sunset without a morsel of food! That was enough to break down the strongest man.

A little before sunset the ominous Cape Railway line stared us in the face. We were again precisely in the same plight as on the 15th of August, when we had to cut the wire near Springfontein Junction, only with this difference—that the danger was much more imminent, the enemy forming a semi-circle at my back, and before me was a line more strongly fenced and better guarded than the first. But happily the armoured train was not on the scene. As we were so successful in our first undertaking, we determined to pass the enemy's line again in daylight. In fine, we had to cut the wire or surrender. The latter was more repulsive than the former.

As my commando was now very near the line, there was not a moment to lose. The enemy was advancing swiftly, and the armoured train might appear at any time. Commandant Louis Wessels, Veldt Cornet Fraser, Landman and myself proceeded with the utmost speed ahead of the commando to cut the wire, in order that the progress of the commando should not be impeded in the least.

As we approached the line a sharp cross-fire from the block-houses was directed against us; but we all reached the fence safely and began cutting the wire as quickly as possible.

The enemy, knowing only too well who were trying to cut the wire, poured volley after volley upon us. The bullets seemed to strike everywhere and everything but ourselves. Let the reader imagine himself exposed to such a fire, between two forts about 800 yards apart on a level track of ground, and forming there in the centre a target for rifles, and he will realise, to some extent, our situation at that moment. But this was not all. To intensify our peril we met with thick steel wire which the scissors refused to cut. We were delayed; the whole commando arrived, and was checked by this wire.

What an embarrassment! I ordered the men to spread, dismount, and fire at the blockhouses until we had done the cutting. This was promptly done. Having, been exposed to the enemy's fire for some minutes, we succeeded at last in cutting that wire also. I then signalled the men to pass. And once more the incredible occurred. On a plain between blockhouses 800 yards apart, exposed to an incessant cross-fire, all the burghers passed the line, in broad daylight, without receiving so much as a scratch. Some horses were shot down, others were wounded, but the men crossed safely. Some distance from the line Lieutenant Bolding was wounded mortally.

I waited at the line till all, with the exception of eight or ten whose horses had given in, were over and then followed the commando. But looking back once more, I beheld one of my men trudging on foot across the line. At once I decided to go back and lend him a helping hand. I rode back, and was again exposed to the same fire from which we had just escaped. This time there was to be no escape. While returning, one of my officers—Fraser—who saw me going back, came to volunteer his services. He would not have me exposed to the enemy's fire, and urged me to go back immediately—he would see to the burgher.

Accepting his generous offer, I rode back. But no sooner had I turned my horse, than I felt a shock. In the twinkling of an eye a bullet had passed through the muscles of my left arm and through my lungs, missing the heart by a mere hair-breadth. It happened all so suddenly that for the first few seconds I hardly knew that I was wounded. I remained in the saddle for a time, until some of the men could attend to me. Gently they took me from my horse, placed me in a blanket, and carried me along to a safe spot.

It was now eventide, the shadows were deepening, and darkness was hiding us from the vision of the foe. At first I was determined to accompany the commando some distance from the line to a place where I could safely remain till recovered. I, however, soon realised the serious nature of the wound, and that if it were not well attended to, mortification was sure to set in, and that would cost me my life. The men too considered it absolutely impossible for me to accompany them any longer, and deemed it advisable that I should be sent into the British hospital for medical treatment.

And then came the *parting* moment, the moment when I had to bid adieu to the men whom I had led, and with whom I had fought against our common foe for so long a time. In the life of every man there comes a day, an hour, or even a moment, which he never can forget. That parting moment, reader, was one in my life I never shall forget. My officers, adjutants, secretary, and some other burghers gathered round me for the last time as I sat on the ground supported by one of them. As they bade me farewell—yea, perhaps for ever—the tear-drops sparkled in their eyes, and gushed down their cheeks. Yes, we all did weep and shed tears of deep sorrow—tears not such as "angels weep," but such as men can weep who love one another, and had fought in one common cause.

I could not speak to the men as I would, for I was too weak. Still I wished them God-speed for the future, and exhorted them to be very courageous and to do their duty faithfully, as befits men, to the last. I told them my work was done. I had given my blood, and might be called upon to give my life for my country. If so, I hope to be prepared to bring that offering too. More I could not do. My secretary then knelt and commended me in prayer to the care and protection of our gracious God and Father.... Then we parted.

My war career had ended. No more fighting, no more retreating, no more roaming over the veldt, by day and night, exposed to blasting summer winds or chilling winter frosts. For two years and two months I had seen active service. During that time I had tried to acquit myself conscientiously of my duties as a man. No sacrifice was too great, and no obstacle appeared insuperable for the cause in which I was engaged. Looking back upon the past I observe how often I have fallen short and failed—failed as a burgher and as a leader. And though I do not wish for another war, I believe I should try to do better were I to live through it again.

Two of my adjutants—Pieter Hugo and Landman—had remained with me. One of them instantly went to the nearest railway station, about three miles off, to call for an ambulance. Till 1 A.M. I lay bleeding in the veldt. Then the British ambulance arrived. When the doctor saw me he had very little hope that I would recover. As I was too weak to be removed by waggon, I was put on a stretcher and carried to a small field hospital, not far from the spot where I was wounded.

How soon I knew that I was no more a free man! First of all I was stripped of all my belongings, including watch, chain, and money, etc. At my urgent request the watch and chain and also a certain amount of my money were restored to me.

The following morning an ambulance train took me to Naauwpoort Junction. On the way I had to part with my blanket. And one of the nurses actually wanted my ring, saying that I might as well give it to her, as it would be taken from me. This I refused to part with, remarking that I didn't believe any one would act so shamefully as to rob me of my ring. In this I was correct.

Arrived at Naauwpoort, I was carried to the hospital, where I was laid up for three weeks. A screen was posted before my bed, and at my feet stood a sentinel with fixed bayonet. I was to be completely isolated from the rest of mankind. Imagine my feelings at having this functionary at my feet, watching over me and staring in my face day and night. It was enough to drive me mad. When I could endure it no longer I entreated one of the sisters to offer my guard a seat, somewhere out of my view, for his penetrating and unbroken gaze was putting too great a strain on my already shattered nerves. Surely there was no chance whatsoever for me to escape, for I could hardly move myself. Besides, the hospital was so well fenced in and strongly guarded, that all escape was impossible. My request was partly granted; but I was forbidden to speak to any one, except to the nurses and the doctor. Neither was any one allowed to address me. And so the time dragged on heavily and wearily. The first few days I suffered intensely, gradually the pain decreased, and I became stronger.

After I had spent three weeks in the hospital I was ordered to Graaff Reinet. I rose, and dressed with the assistance of the nurses. To my astonishment six khakis entered my room. One of these had a pair of handcuffs. To my query as to what his intentions were he replied: "You must be handcuffed." "Well, and where do you want to put them on?" I asked him, for my wounded arm was still supported by a sling. "I must put them on somewhere," he replied bluntly. So I suggested that I would lie down on the stretcher and have them fastened to my feet. I was beginning to lose my temper, and expressed myself in somewhat forcible language. Fortunately an officer then appeared on the scene with whom I remonstrated about the treatment I was being subjected to. The officer, shrugging his shoulders, said: "'Tis orders, and they must be executed." It seemed such a disgraceful action that I could not help remarking: "That is why the Boers will not surrender. If wounded officers, entrusted to your care, are treated thus, what must the private expect?" At last I was allowed to go—unhandcuffed.

Placed in an armoured truck, I was taken to Graaff Reinet Gaol. My experiences there shall be related in the next chapter. Had I suffered much up to this time, greater suffering and more anxious moments were awaiting me.

Before leaving this subject I would sincerely thank the doctors and sisters, who evinced such great interest and attended so well to my case while laid up in the Naauwpoort Hospital.

CHAPTER VII

COURT-MARTIALLED

O, if to fight for ... commonweal
Were piety in thine, it is in these....
Wilt thou draw near the nature of the Gods?
Draw near them then in being merciful.

—*Shakespeare*

Arrived at Graaff Reinet, I was instantly removed to gaol, where I was confined in a small room. Here, isolated from the rest of the world, I was to spend many anxious days and sleepless nights. During the day I was allowed to stay a few hours in an inner yard or enclosure of the prison. The rest of the time I was locked up, and no bright sun-rays could revive my drooping spirits. I begged permission to go as far as the prisoner's yard, and promised not to speak to the other prisoners—no, not even wink an eye, and should I transgress in any respect the guard could shoot me down. I desired intensely to move and breathe in the open and pure air—Nature's gift to all. But this favour was too great. On the contrary, I was forbidden, on penalty of death, to address any one. To add to my misery other forces seemed to co-operate. For the very evening after my arrival an unknown gentleman entered my room. He carried some documents, and politely informed me that I must get ready for my trial. He hinted, moreover, that I should expect the worst. If I had not a will, and wanted one, it should be drawn up without further delay. If I had any documents to be disposed of, I should arrange about these as well. In short, this kind (?) fellow gave me to understand that my career was soon to terminate. How? That was the question.

The next morning the local magistrate came to pay me his respects. The unpleasant remarks of the previous evening were cruelly reiterated, enlarged upon, and emphasized. The magistrate volunteered very kindly to submit, if necessary, all my papers to some one I may please to appoint. He would also deliver messages to my sorrowing friends and relatives. As my trial was pending, I asked him what he meant by talking such nonsense. Surely the British were not going to shoot each and every Boer officer whom they captured, and that without fair trial!

Though no coward, I must admit that such conversations were not calculated to produce a favourable impression on my mind. They might have been well meant, but did more harm than good. It is one thing to face the enemy on the battlefield, where one may defend himself; 'tis something else to be dangerously, almost mortally, wounded, and then to be at the mercy of the foe. For three consecutive nights Nature's greatest gift—sleep—to suffering humanity had departed from me. Why could I not sleep? Was it fear that kept me awake? No, not that. My conscience was clear, my hands unstained. But locked up in that small room, with no one to speak to, my thoughts began to multiply, and I lay meditating night after night. That was enough to make a young man old and grey. Yet there was one friend who helped me to beguile the dreary hours of confinement. That friend was my beloved pipe.

One evening, towards the end of February, I was told to appear before a military court the following morning. This announcement seemed strange to me, for I was not prepared for a trial. I was resolved what to do.

At 8 o'clock the next morning I was taken by an escort of six soldiers to the court-house. Having taken my place in the prisoner's box, I listened to my charges, which were recited as follows: Fourteen cases of murder; wreckage of trains; and ill-treatment of prisoners-of-war. To the question, "Guilty or not?" I pleaded "Not guilty," whereupon I was requested to make my defence, which I declined to do; for the public prosecutor had promised me, and rightly so, that, if I could produce any witnesses to disprove the [alleged] charges brought against me, I could summon them. As none of my witnesses were present, nor an opportunity of enlisting the services of an advocate and solicitor given me, I refused to take upon me the burden of pleading in self-defence. I knew that if I did acquiesce in such a trial, it might prove fatal to my best interests. It would then be urged, too, that Kritzinger had a fair trial, when condemned to death, something which would be altogether untrue.

After I had thrice declined to be tried without witnesses and legal advice, I was sent to gaol, and told to be ready for trial on the 7th of March. I now addressed a letter to General French, in which I brought to his notice how I was being treated. French wrote back that he had corresponded with Lord Kitchener concerning my case, and that Lord Kitchener's orders were that I should have a fair trial, *i.e.*, legal defence and witnesses for my case.

On the 1st of March, seven days before the appointed trial, I was again summoned to appear in court. My charges were read out, and the same questions were submitted to me. Again I declined to make a defence, and remarked: "I am in your power, gentlemen—you may do as you please, pronounce any sentence; but *I* shall *not* defend myself." I then referred the court to French's letter, whereupon I was again removed to my lodgings.

Meanwhile, I succeeded in enlisting the services of Advocate Gardiner and Attorney Auret, Graaff Reinet, and made such arrangements that my witnesses could be present at the trial.

Advocate Gardiner arrived on the evening of the 6th of March. The following day the court-martial commenced. As my witnesses had not yet arrived, it was decided that the evidence for the prosecution should first be taken.

The counsel for the defence took exception to the charges of train-wreckage, ill-treatment of troops, and some instances of murder; charges which, *prima facie*, would not stand the test of examination. These were then withdrawn by the prosecution. After this subtraction there still remained four charges of murder, which we shall enumerate in succession.

1st Charge:—

Murder.

On or about the 15th of February, 1901, it was alleged that I had killed and murdered Jafta and Solomon, natives, British subjects, at Grootplaats, Murraysburg, Cape Colony.

Mr. Boltman, the owner of the farm Grootplaats, was the principal witness for the prosecution. He deposed that he saw one of my officers, *i.e.*, Antonie Wessels, riding up to me, and after Wessels had spoken to me he rode back and shot the two natives. Hence I must have given him orders to shoot them! Besides, Mr. Boltman also declared that he had heard me say to two men, whom I had arrested along with the two natives in question, "Do you see these natives? Well, I am going to have them shot, and in future I shall treat all armed natives in the same way." All these statements were refuted by one of the men to whom I was supposed to have made the remark of having the natives shot. The man denied that he ever heard such a statement from my lips.

2nd Charge:—

Murder.

In that I have killed and murdered John Vondeling, a native and British subject, at Tweefontein, Graaff Reinet.

In this case it was proved by the witnesses for the defence that the native had been shot three days before my arrival at the farm where the murder was committed.

3rd Charge:—

Murder.

About the 18th of March, 1901, I had killed and brutally murdered a native at Prinsfontein, Tarkastad.

Mr. Mantel, the farmer, deposed:—

> One of Kritzinger's men was with me as his commando passed some distance from my house. Van der Walt said to me, "Do you see that man in front, riding on the large blue horse? That man is Kritzinger." I then saw a few burghers riding up to Kritzinger, and after they had halted for a short while they went back and shot the natives.

My witnesses proved that at that particular time I had no blue horse in my possession. Neither was there such a man as Van der Walt in my commando; and the natives in question had been shot by another commandant without my instructions.

4th Charge:—

Murder.

At Biscuitfontein, Bethulie, I had killed and murdered two natives on the 14th of August, 1901.

This was the last and principal charge brought against me. Four blacks were the chief witnesses in this case, by which, if possible, I was to be convicted and silenced for ever.

Let us see how they fared. The first one succeeded in identifying me. The next one was less successful. He pointed to an English officer, saying, "That is the man." He was to have another chance. I looked at him and smiled; this puzzled him even more. Greatly perplexed, he pressed his finger against a man with a long bushy beard, and said, "You are Kritzinger." What a blunder! The prosecutor seemed slightly put out; the court indulged in lusty laughter.

The other witnesses were then brought forward. Surely these will not make a mistake, they know the murderer only too well. Had the prosecutor not sounded them beforehand by asking them to point out the prisoner's photo among a number of other photos? Did they not hit upon the right photo? Is this not conclusive evidence that they must have seen and known the prisoner? In spite of all this precaution, the first witness in this case declared, on being cross-questioned *re* the photo in question, that a certain officer had shown him the photo at Norval's Pont, and asked him to note it carefully, so that, if called upon, he would be able to identify the person concerned!

I watched the prosecutor, who exhibited signs of uneasiness or disgust. This stupid native was spoiling his good case; the other witness was going to commit as great a blunder. He declared that on the 10th of January he saw the corpses of two natives, and, on seeing them, immediately recognized the one as being the body of his brother-in-law. Questioned as to how he could still recognize his brother-in-law in a decomposed body, he promptly replied, "Oh! my brother had still a smile on his face!" Although the native in question was shot on the 14th of August, 1901, on the 10th of January he still had a smile on his face! Death must have conferred a great boon upon him. And if he could have appeared in court, he certainly would have objected to my being tried. Have not sentences of death, confiscation of property, and imprisonment been passed on the evidences of such witnesses?

When all the evidences had been taken the prosecutor delivered his address. After him the counsel for the defence addressed the court. In a very able speech Advocate Gardiner pointed out the shallowness of the accusations against me. He urged that the court should not be long in coming to a decision, as a prolonged trial meant increased expenses for the accused.

After his address I was removed for half an hour. Summoned back, a verdict of "not guilty" was brought in. I was at last acquitted, and could return to my lonely chamber not as a criminal, but as a prisoner-of-war!

Leaving the court-room I was called back to shake hands with the judges, who congratulated me with the acquittal. Thus the trial, which lasted five days, came to an end. The clouds cleared up. The sun rose. It was all brightness. I had passed unscathed through the ordeal, to indulge that night in slumbers calm and sweet.

Just a few days before the trial commenced I was somewhat reassured and encouraged to hope for the best. An unknown friend kindly dropped a newspaper cutting, tied to a piece of stone, over the prison yard. This press-cutting fell into my hands, and in it I saw that a large section of the British public strongly disapproved of the action of the Military Government *re* late Commandant Scheepers, and that section and people all over the continent and in the United States of America were asking, "What about Kritzinger—will he too be shot?" I noticed also that petitions on my behalf were being drawn up in England and elsewhere, and signed extensively.

All the men and women who so petitioned His Majesty the King to spare my life I thank most sincerely, for the interest shown in my case, and for the efforts put forth to save my life. How much I owe such I do not fully know; but I do appreciate the deed of kindness shown to me in the darkest moments of my life. Such deeds are never forgotten. They illuminate life's way with such splendour as fills the soul with inexpressible gratitude.

I have related the story of my trial briefly and as accurately as I could. I do not wish to comment on the justice or injustice of the proceedings. It is for others to judge whether an officer, who was a burgher of the Orange Free State, and *not* a rebel, should have been court-martialled, and while the war was still in progress, on such unfounded charges. I shall not say whether I consider it just and fair that, tried as a prisoner-of-war and acquitted as such, I should have had to pay a bill of L226 for my defence. What if a prisoner does not possess the means to secure legal defence? Must he then be condemned without it? Has this not been done in certain cases? I shall ask no more questions. I did not mind the money, but was only too glad to inhale once more air not pregnant with death and destruction.

Our object in mentioning these details is to illustrate the nature of some of the charges brought against Boer officers and burghers when court-martialled by the British. These charges of murder were, as a rule, associated with Kaffirs who had been shot, either in fair fight or as spies. Our officers were held responsible for the acts of their men. Moreover, by proclamation, any officer or burgher convicted of shooting a Kaffir or Hottentot, after having surrendered, could be charged with murder and condemned to death. The principle laid down in this proclamation, that the life of a surrendered foe should not be taken, must be endorsed by every right-minded man. The burghers, however, argued that, since the war had not been declared against the coloured races, they had the right to deal with armed natives in the most effectual manner possible, especially if these natives were not British subjects, but belonged to the Republics. Besides, some of these natives gave no quarter to our men. We could cite several instances where burghers had been murdered and mutilated in a ghastly manner. To mention one instance, while peace negotiations were going on, 56 men were savagely cut up and mutilated by the Kaffirs in the district of Vryheid, Transvaal.

Eventually we were placed in such a position that we hardly knew what to do with armed natives. What if they refuse to surrender? Shoot them ... and then you are a murderer. Let them go ... and then you will pay the penalty. It was perplexing to know how the British wished us to act. The Boers, regardless of consequences, did what they thought right.

For the sake of such as were interested in my trial, I submit in full the charges, my evidence, and the addresses of the prosecutor and counsel for the defence:—

Charge Sheet.

The prisoner, Pieter Hendrik Kritzinger, a burgher of the late Orange Free State, and ex-Assistant Chief Commandant of the (so-called) Federal forces, is charged with:—

1st Charge:—

Murder.

In that he, at Grootplaats, Murraysburg, on or about the 15th of February, 1901, killed and murdered Jafta and Solomon, natives, British subjects.

2nd Charge:—

Murder.

In that he, at Tweefontein, Graaff Reinet, on or about the 15th of February, 1901, killed and murdered John Thomas, a native, a British subject.

3rd Charge:—

Murder.

In that he, at Prinsfontein, Tarkastad, on or about the 18th of March, 1901, killed and murdered a native, a British subject.

4th Charge:—

Murder.

In that he, at Biscuitfontein, Bethulie, Orange River Colony, on or about the 15th of August, 1901, killed and murdered Koos and Willem, natives, British subjects.

5th Charge:—

Destroying Railways.

In that he, near Knutsford, Cradock, on or about the 27th of July, 1901, cut the railway line, thereby causing a portion of a passenger train to be derailed.

To be tried by Military Court by order of General French.

The prisoner takes his stand at the place from which other witnesses give their evidence:—

The prisoner, Pieter Hendrik Kritzinger, being duly sworn, states:—

"My name is Pieter Hendrik Kritzinger. In the commencement of September, 1900, I became a commandant of the Free State Forces. I became Chief Commandant of the forces in the Cape Colony on the 11th of June, 1901. This would not give me a higher position in the event of my returning to the Free State. Once over the border I would hold the same position as any other commandant. I surrendered on the 16th of December last. I attempted to cross the line at Hanover Road and was wounded.

I know absolutely nothing of the death of Jafta and Solomon, I gave no orders that they should be shot, nor any other natives. I arrived at Voetpad on a Thursday, the 14th of February, 1901. I camped there until the following day. Shortly before I left Voetpad Captain Smit with his men came there from a farm in the vicinity. The name of the farm is unknown to me. Captain Smit was not under my command. He was acting independently. An advance guard is generally sent out. On this occasion I sent Wessels and some men. I do not know when Wessels left,

I cannot remember. I went from Voetpad to Poortje, the farm of Van der Merwe. I arrived there about sundown on Friday the 15th. On my way from Voetpad I passed over Boltman's place. I did not hear of any natives being shot there. While on Voetpad I had no message from Wessels. I cannot remember having spoken to any one in that strain regarding Boltman's statements *re* shooting natives. There was one Mijnhardt in my commando, there were others amongst Smit's men, but I can't call to mind of a Corporal Mijnhardt in my commando. No report was ever made to me of natives being shot at Grootplaats.

2nd Charge:—

On the 15th of February, 1901, I went to Poortje. I camped there for the night. On the 16th I went to Driefontein, the farm of du Toit. That was Saturday. From there I went on Sunday to the farm Tweefontein, Minnaar's. I have not had a man named Van Aswegen with me at Minnaar's. I know a Van Aswegen; he is a sergeant in Smit's commando. He was not at Minnaar's when I got there. I do not know where he was. On the 12th of February, 1901, I saw Van Aswegen on a farm, the name of which is unknown to me. The owner's name is Burger. There Smit and his men left me. I next saw Van Aswegen on a farm in the Richmond district, the owner of which is Meiring. I stopped at Minnaar's for the day, held service, and left there in the afternoon. I know nothing of the shooting of a native there. No shooting of a native was reported to me. Van Aswegen certainly had no orders from me. He was not under my control, he was under the control of Smit. Nobody belonging to my commando had any orders from me with reference to shooting natives.

3rd Charge:—

The Court does not think it necessary to take the prisoner's evidence on this charge.

4th Charge:—

I crossed the Orange River into the Orange River Colony on or about the 15th of August last. It is brought back to my memory inasmuch as Commandant Cachet was killed on the 15th of August in the district of Venterstad in the Cape Colony. I did not take any natives prisoner prior to crossing the river. Commandant Wessels was with me before I got to the river, about five or six miles from the river he left me and crossed. I crossed the Orange River on the Bethulie side. Wessels crossed the river on the Norval's Pont side. I did not see him cross the river. After crossing I went to the first farm. No one was at home there, and I off-saddled. The name of the farm is unknown to me. It was a farm that had been burnt. When I arrived at that farm there was no other commando there. Before I crossed the river I heard rifle-fire, but after I had off-saddled for a little while I heard cannon-fire. The firing came from the west, from the direction which Wessels had crossed the river. The cannon-firing also came from the same direction.

I mounted a horse and rode up a kopje to see if I could see anything that might be taking place. The kopje was about 1,000 to 1,200 yards from my laager. I was riding a chestnut horse. I went to the kopje alone, but a man by the name of Michael Coetzee, whom I intend to call as a witness, was on the kopje on duty as a sentinel. I remained there a considerable time. I saw cannon-firing on a little ridge on the Colony side of the river. I heard rifle-fire while I was on the kopje. I returned to the laager. The firing was in the direction of the laager. When I got back to the laager Commandant Wessels was there, off-saddled. After I arrived at the camp I spoke to him about the firing I had heard. I knew that some of the farmer's cattle were being brought in for the purpose of slaughtering, and I asked Wessels why they fired so many shots at the animals, and he replied that a couple of Kaffirs had been shot. I was chaffing Wessels when I asked him why they fired so many shots at the animals. When I was on the kopje I certainly did not know that Wessels had taken natives prisoner. I did not see these natives after they had been shot. I do not know the boy Jan Louw. I did not speak to him that day, nor to any other native. The Wessels in question is the Commandant Louis Wessels, who passed into the Colony from the Orange River Colony, and I met him three or four days before I crossed. The day after our meeting we had a skirmish with the British. Wessels and I got separated. The following day we met again on the farm of Van der Keever. He was not under my command in the Colony, nor in the Orange River Colony. I had about between seventy and eighty men when I crossed the river, and Wessels had between thirty and forty men. I had a few natives shot in the Orange River Colony prior to my crossing into the Colony in the first instance. These were tried by Captain Scheepers, Captain Fouche, and Captain Smit and myself, also Judge Hugo. The papers were sent to Assistant Chief Commandant Fourie, and the sentences were approved of by him. That was the only case of natives having been shot by me.

Prosecutor's Address.

(Captain L. Daine.)

"As regards the first charge, the natives Jafta and Solomon and the scouts McCabe and Maasdorp were captured by Wessels, who was in charge of Kritzinger's scouts. He took them to Grootplaats. McCabe proves that Wessels then went towards Voetpad, three miles off, and returned some time afterwards, gave an order to his men, and the two natives were led off to execution. Boltman's statements that Kritzinger gave a message for British column commanders, informing them that armed natives would be shot, are fully corroborated by what McCabe was told by members of Kritzinger's commando, and clearly shows Kritzinger's intentions and instructions. Kritzinger states that he cannot remember whether he gave the message or not.

"The witnesses for the defence all state that there were no prisoners with the commando at Grootplaats, yet the accuracy with which they describe different horses, and the date of seeing Van Aswegen, *i.e.*, 13th February, 1901, is little short of marvellous. Kritzinger states that he mounted a horse and rode to the kopje, which was about 1,000 to 1,200 yards from the laager, and that he was riding a chestnut horse, while the witnesses for the defence state that he was riding a dark bay horse with a star when he rode to the kopje.

"As regards the natives mentioned in the first charge, McCabe states that he did not lose sight of them all the time they were together, and as they were not searched in his presence the passes could therefore not have been found. They were captured on a farm in British territory.

"As regards the second charge, Van Aswegen was evidently a member of Kritzinger's commando, and the witness, Van der Merwe, remembers seeing him with the commando for three weeks, during which time he and his men were frequently away. Here again, as concerns spies, Van Aswegen had the passes in his hand and knew what the boy really was.

"As regards the fourth charge, the natives were captured in the Cape Colony, where Kritzinger was Chief Commandant. The statement that his authority as such ceased the moment he crossed the Orange River is hardly credible. The natives were shot at Biscuitfontein, where Kritzinger was laagered at the time, and their dead bodies were seen by de Klerk there. Jan Louw is very clear as to who the commandant was. He recognized his photo on two occasions, and identified him at once in court. The dark brown horse ridden by Kritzinger to the kopje is probably the black referred to, and his evidence is corroborated by Jan Jonkers, who, however, failed to recognize Kritzinger in court, more through fright than anything else, I think. Both these witnesses state that there was a body of men at Biscuitfontein when they arrived. This is denied by witnesses for the defence. The bodies found by Jan Hans must have been those of Koos and Willem, as the spot is identified as that described by de Klerk.

"It must be remembered that the witnesses Hugo, Matthijsen, Van Wijk and de Klerk are all accomplices, and therefore their evidence must be received with caution, especially after the curiously minute details they give on some points. It is also worthy of note that Matthijsen was not examined on the fourth charge, though he was present with Kritzinger at the time.

"The shooting of these prisoners was absolutely unjustifiable and illegal, and all concerned must be held equally responsible.

"Wessels took over the command of Kritzinger's commando when the latter was wounded.

"As regards the proclamation, the only name mentioned in

it is that of Kritzinger, and the proclamation is signed by him. The names of any of the other commandants are not mentioned in it at all.

"As regards the witnesses for the prosecution, there are three who have been deported, and therefore could not be obtained."

Address by the Counsel for the Defence.

(Advocate H.G. Gardiner.)

"Mr. President and Members of the Military Court:—

"We are now reaching the end of a great trial, the great trial of a great man. Of all the trials that have been held before Military Courts in this country, this, I may fairly say, is most important.

"No officer of higher or even equal rank to him, who was once Chief Commandant in this Colony, has yet been tried, and on this trial much will depend. It is a case the result of which may have great and far-reaching influence. It may influence greatly the Boer commandoes in the field. On the verdict now given in his case the attitude of other leaders will greatly depend. I do not urge this upon you that you should acquit the prisoner. I do not ask you to consider the consequences of the verdict you may bring in. I know that you will bring in whatever verdict you think right regardless of all consequences, but I do bring these facts before you as a reason why you should carefully consider the evidence.

"The charge in this case is the charge of murder, the greatest crime that can be brought against a man. It is a crime of which a man cannot be technically guilty. You must have the most convincing evidence before you, and the clearest proof. It is a crime where intent must be clearly proved; where intent is essential. A merchant whose agent enters into a contract may be held responsible to carry out that contract, but a merchant whose clerk commits a crime cannot be held responsible for that crime. It would, sir, be intolerable if a leader of a column should be held responsible for every act committed by the men under his command. We are glad to know, sir, that in the history of this war British troops have behaved in an exemplary manner, but there have been occasions when they have done things not in accordance with the laws and usages of war, and it would be unfair to hold a general responsible for such acts of isolated individuals. On the question of intent and what constitutes responsibility for a crime, I would refer to *Manual of Military Law*, pages 112 and 113, paragraph 17:—'If the offence charged involves some special intent, it must be shown that the assistant was cognizant of the intention of the person whom he assisted; thus, on a charge of wounding with intent to murder, it must be shown that the assistant not only assisted the principal offender in what he did, but also knew what his intention was, before the former can be convicted on the full charge.' Then again, paragraph 18. After referring to persons going out with common intent it says that a person is not responsible for any offence 'committed by any member of the party, which is unconnected with a common purpose, unless he personally instigates or assists in its commission.' And to give an example, sir, of common intent, the purpose for which a commander and his men go on commando is to kill and destroy the enemy, not that of killing prisoners and non-combatants, or prisoners without a trial, and if a subordinate without orders from his superior commits a crime, that superior cannot be held responsible for it unless he has consented to it or knew of it. I would also refer to paragraph 20:—'Mere knowledge that a person is about to commit an offence, and even conduct influenced by such knowledge, will not make a person responsible for that offence, unless he does something actively to encourage its commission.' And last of all I would refer to Army Act, section 6, page 322:—'Every person subject to Military Law who commits any of the following offences, that is to say (*f*):—Does violence to any person bringing provisions or supplies to the forces, or commits any offence against the property of persons or any inhabitant or resident in the country in which he is serving,' but says nothing about the responsibility of a superior officer.

"We may take it therefore that Kritzinger can only be responsible for a murder when he has given either general or special orders, or when he knew of it beforehand, and consented to its being done. Now, sir, what proof have we of that being so in this case?

"Let us take the first charge—the charge of shooting two natives at Grootplaats. There can be no doubt that these natives were spies. They came into the Boer lines unarmed, ununiformed, and with false passes. They carried two passes, one representing them as belonging to the 7th Dragoon Guards, and the other to the effect that they were looking for cattle. I think if such a case came before you, you would have no doubts about treating them as spies. Therefore Kritzinger would not have been guilty of murder had he shot them. I have a far stronger defence, however. The natives were captured by Wessels. Kritzinger knew nothing about them, and when these boys were shot he was not present, as he was at another farm at the time. Wessels left at 10 A.M., Kritzinger arrived there after sunset. How can he then be responsible for the shooting of these natives when he was not at the farm? There is not a bit of proof to show that Kritzinger gave the order about the shooting of these boys. One of the native witnesses says that one of Wessels' men went in the direction of Voetpad; there is no evidence that he ever reached there. More than that, witnesses belonging to Kritzinger's commando state that they saw nothing of Wessels, and that they knew nothing of the shooting of these boys. At the close of the evidence in chief there was something which looked like implicating Kritzinger, but of that by Van Aswegen there is very little left to-day. At first the evidence *re* Mijnhardt was taken, but the Court has ruled that this evidence cannot be accepted. Now there is the evidence of Boltman. I do not say that Boltman did not give his evidence fairly, but he must have made a mistake as regards Kritzinger making use of the words he referred to. McCabe says while he was on the farm nothing of the kind occurred. If anything had been said he would have heard it. When McCabe and Maasdorp came back no report was made that Kritzinger had said anything of the kind. But there was a report made, and McCabe bears it out that something was said by another member of the commando. I would submit that Boltman mistook the other member of the commando for Kritzinger. There is no getting over the evidence of McCabe, and he is the person who ought to remember it. As McCabe says, Kritzinger did not arrive until some hours after the boys had been shot.

"I now come to the second charge—the charge of the shooting of the boy John Thomas at Tweefontein. Now, sir, here again the boy was clearly a spy. He carried two passes similar to those carried by the boys mentioned in the first charge. He was unarmed. He was not in uniform. He was there to spy the movements of the Boers. Kritzinger would not have been responsible for the shooting of this boy had he shot him. But here the evidence against him is even weaker than in the first charge. Here there is no suggestion that the boy was shot by any of Kritzinger's men. The evidence shows that the boy was shot by a man serving under Smit. Smit was an officer with an independent command, and, more than that, he had been longer in service than Kritzinger himself, and was not under Kritzinger. Here, too, there is no suggestion, as in the first charge, that any message was taken to Kritzinger by the men who shot this boy, John Thomas. None of Van Aswegen's men were sent to Kritzinger. Van Aswegen himself did not go back. No one from Kritzinger came to Van Aswegen. Van Aswegen was last seen by Kritzinger on the 12th or 13th of February, 1901, and was not seen again by him until a couple of days after the shooting.

"That the boy was shot by Van Aswegen appears clear from the two Minnaars' evidence, who say that the boy was taken out by Van Aswegen, and that was the last they saw of him. Kritzinger did not arrive until Sunday morning with his commando, and everyone says he knows absolutely nothing about the shooting of the native. I would submit that there is absolutely nothing to connect Kritzinger with the shooting of this boy.

"On the 3rd Charge there is no need to say anything. The Court has already indicated that it is unnecessary to proceed further with it.

"I now come to the 4th Charge; the only charge in which Kritzinger was said to have been present at the shooting. In the first two charges, Kritzinger did not appear until hours after the natives had been shot. The only witnesses who say that Kritzinger was present at the shooting of the natives mentioned in this charge are natives. There appear to have been no white men present. Some one said that Schmidt was present, but it appears he did not cross the river. We have only native evidence to this effect, and native evidence is most unreliable, and only one of the witnesses could identify Kritzinger. We are, therefore, driven back to the evidence of Jan Louw. Even if Jan Louw had given his evidence in a way that could not be shaken, it would be dangerous to convict on the evidence of one witness alone. Natives have no idea of dates, time, or distances. They find it difficult to identify prisoners. We have seen that in the case of Jan Jonkers, and that shows how much reliance can be placed on native evidence. Jan Jonkers identifies a man in Court as being Kritzinger who was never near the place. Four months after a man has been killed Jan Hans goes and sees his body. He identifies him not by the clothes he wears but by his face. Is it possible that after being for four months on the plains of the Orange Free State, exposed to the air and the heat, a man could identify the face of another? And the one native witness is the witness Jan Louw. Even if Jan Louw were a strong witness, his evidence would not have been sufficient to convict, but Jan Louw's evidence falls to the ground under cross-examination. How did Jan Louw identify Kritzinger? He was taken to the office at Norval's Pont. Now, Jan Louw had only seen one commandant in his life. When in that commandant's possession, his life was apparently not worth very much. His companions were shot. When shown any commandant's photo he would naturally identify it with the commandant he knew. Now, Jan Jonkers explains to us why the photo was identified. He was asked, 'Is that Kritzinger?' and he replied, 'That is Kritzinger.' Now, a native is very likely, in a case like that, to say, 'That is the man.' Then Jan Jonkers, in re-examination, tries to get out of that. He says that he said, 'That is Kritzinger,' and then the man in the office said, 'That is Kritzinger.' The probability is that Jan Louw and Jan Jonkers were asked if it was Kritzinger's photo, and they said, 'Yes.' If the Court saw the photos they could see how much reliance could be placed on the identification. The witnesses were taken into a room where there were several groups of photos, but the biggest photo was that of Kritzinger, and these natives had seen it before. Probably it is the only photo they have seen in their lives. It was the same photo they had seen at Norval's Pont. What would one expect? One would naturally expect them to pick out that photo, and that is what occurred. Well, after that, one can understand why Jan Louw identifies Kritzinger in Court. He has had a photo shown to him in town, and of course he naturally identifies Kritzinger at once. The wonder is that Jan Jonkers did not identify Kritzinger. It only shows what small reliance can be placed on the evidence of natives, and that is the sole evidence on which the 4th Charge is based.

"Now let us see what Kritzinger's story is. It is a consistent story, and it seems what probably happened under the circumstances. He crossed without prisoners, and everyone in his commando bears him out. He crossed before Wessels, and laagered there, and afterwards Wessels came up. Jan Louw says that no other commando was there when he arrived, and no other came afterwards. Jan Jonkers says there were about one hundred men when he arrived. The Court will have no doubt that there were two commandoes there. Kritzinger said that he had seventy or eighty men with him. And then again we have Jan Jonkers. If Jan Jonkers found a commando there, all the evidence goes to show that Jan Jonkers must have been with Wessels, and not with Kritzinger. Wessels captured these men, and therefore must have done the shooting.

"Then there is the question of identifying a horse. Both natives say it was a black horse, and the other evidence shows it was a chestnut horse. It may appear strange that our men remember the horses, but I would certainly trust any Boer, who has to deal with horses all his life, rather than a native. Then Kritzinger says he left the commando and went up to the kopje. Wessels had not arrived yet, and that, sir, is borne out by every one of Kritzinger's witnesses; and, as he says, and all the witnesses say, it was in Kritzinger's absence that Wessels arrived and the shooting was done. Kritzinger says he heard the shots and chaffed Wessels about an ox he supposed they were shooting. But whatever was done in Kritzinger's absence was done entirely without Kritzinger's knowledge, and, sir, by men who belonged to Wessels, because whoever did the shooting it was done by men belonging to the commando who took these natives prisoners. Now, sir, it is unfortunate that the witness who was with Kritzinger on the kopje, and who could also have heard the shots, is not here. I know it is not the fault of the Court that he is not here. It is unfortunate, though, that this man is in St. Helena. But Kritzinger is already corroborated by his other witnesses, and against them is only a single native witness. There is, of course, this story of a conversation between Kritzinger and the boy Jan Louw. Kritzinger is supposed to have said to the boy: 'Did you see those boys? They are to be shot. Put down your billies, and go and be shot also,' and then at once to have changed his mind: 'Never mind, my boy, get the water.' It is an improbable story. Jan Jonkers does not appear to have heard the conversation at all. None of Kritzinger's men appear to know of it, and I submit it was not said by Kritzinger, if said at all. Then on the prosecution's side one native witness is contradicted by all the other witnesses.

"Before I close the case for the defence, I would like to refer to the character of the prisoner. In this case I am well aware that character is not a ground of acquittal. I know, sir, that good men of excellent characters have committed crimes, and I would not for one moment appeal for an acquittal because Kritzinger has behaved so well in other instances, and has shown himself a humane man, and a man of honour. I do not ask for mercy on the ground of Kritzinger's character, we can only ask for a fair and just verdict. But character is of importance when there is any doubt in the case. I ask the Court to bear in mind the character of the accused. Is a man who bears such a character likely to have committed the crimes charged against him? The character of Kritzinger, if we put aside the charges in his case, is an excellent one. The prosecution has brought out in cross-examination a certain proclamation. I am glad it has been brought out, for it goes to show nothing against the character of the accused, but it tells in his favour, for, what do we find? That a draft proclamation was drawn up at a meeting of commandants, at which Kritzinger was chairman. He opposed it by every means in his power, but he was in the minority, and, as president of the gathering, he had to sign it. He then asked for some postponement before that proclamation was circulated, and that was agreed to. He still fought against this proclamation, for he asked that before De Wet approved of it nothing should be done in the way of circulation. He never circulated it himself. If it was circulated, it was done by the other commandants against the agreement. It was not approved of by De Wet, and never became a proclamation. This shows that Kritzinger disapproved of the harsh measures contained in it, that he tried to get it done away with, and that at last he succeeded in getting a refusal from the Chief Commandant of the Free State. It was owing to his efforts that the proclamation did not become a valid one in this Colony, and he cannot be responsible for anything that may have been done against the agreement arrived at by those at the meeting.

"As regards his treatment of natives, he tells you himself that he never had natives shot, except those boys who were duly tried, and whose sentences were duly confirmed, and that will tell in his favour.

"As regards his attitude *re* the destruction of property, we have the letter to Scheepers, and the Court will bear that in mind in deciding whether he has been guilty of these acts of inhumanity charged against him or not.

"His character has been excellent. Coming back into danger again in order to secure a remount for one of his men whose horse had been shot, he was himself wounded, and ultimately captured. His conduct on that occasion was that of a brave man, as it has been all through the war. If there is a question of doubt I ask the Court to bear in mind the character of the prisoner. All the evidence is riddled with doubt, and you have to weigh this, sir. On the one hand the native was shot in Kritzinger's absence. There is no proof that it was done by his order, or with his consent. The evidence of the natives in the 4th Charge is of the weakest description. Against that you have his excellent character, and the story corroborated by his own witnesses and corroborated in some respects by the witnesses for the prosecution. I ask you, sir, to weigh that evidence in the balance, and see which side is found wanting.

"Just a word more, and I have done. I know there are some people who say it is unfair to try a man by a Court composed of men who have been fighting against him. Sir, I have no such fear. I know, sir, I feel sure that there is not an officer in South Africa who would not gladly acquit the prisoner of the crimes laid to his charge if he felt he could conscientiously do so. I therefore leave in your hands the fate of a man whose bravery has been shown on many occasions, in many a hard fight, whose honesty and humanity have been, in many instances, conspicuous. More than that, sir, should he be acquitted, when this war is over, he will, I feel sure, be able and ready to do much to restore the good feeling which we all hope will prevail between English and Dutch, I leave his fate in your hands with the conviction that you will bring in the only verdict warranted by the evidence, a verdict of 'Not guilty.'"

This address gives you, reader, the gist of my trial. If you have had the patience to read through it you will be able to have a fair conception of what we had to pass through in the early days of March, 1902.

CHAPTER VIII

WHY WE SURRENDERED

Breathes there the man, with soul so dead,
Who never to himself hath said,
This is my own, my native land!...
If such there breathe, go, mark him well.

—*Walter Scott*

We shall now direct our attention to some of the disadvantages and difficulties which confronted us in our struggle for freedom. This we do because many who were in sympathy with the Republics have been sorely disappointed in their surrender, and some suppose that they should have prolonged the struggle until victory ultimately crowned their efforts. Those who reason in this way must be ignorant of the conditions of the Republics at the time of their surrender, neither do they know the disadvantages with which we had to grapple throughout the war. It is therefore of importance that the South African War should be regarded in the light and under the circumstances in which it was begun, conducted and concluded. When the obstacles the Boer had to encounter are taken into due consideration, then censure and disappointment vanish and make room for praise and admiration.

None know better than those who have been involved in war that its current does not run evenly. Experience has taught them that war is much more than a series of exciting adventures or some kind of sport. It brings before the contending parties problems hard to solve, difficulties and emergencies of a most perplexing and bewildering nature. Boer and Briton alike had to face such difficulties and disadvantages. The disadvantages, however, under which the English had to labour in South Africa dwindle into insignificance when contrasted and compared with those of the Boers, especially towards the latter part of the war. The impartial critic must admit that eventually the vantage ground was altogether on the side of the British. 'Tis only by sheer determination and superhuman efforts and sacrifices on the part of the late Republics that they defied the British Empire for two years and eight months. None were perhaps more surprised and amazed at the protracted war than the Imperial Government itself. Time and again an early termination of hostilities was announced. Such was the case after Cronje's capture, the occupation of Bloemfontein and Pretoria, and Prinsloo's surrender. When Lord Roberts left South Africa, the war, it was said, was practically over!

The British were placed at a great disadvantage at the outbreak of hostilities. The Boer ultimatum, issued on the 9th of October, 1899, found the English Government only half prepared either to accept or reject its demands. None thought that the Boer Republics would ever take such a bold step, and would be so audacious as to despatch an ultimatum to one of the mightiest Powers of the world. They should have waited and waited until that strong Power was quite prepared to crush them at one stroke. They should have waited, at least, till all the British forces were massed on their borders, then to cross, and take by force what peaceful negotiations failed to obtain. Thus reasoned some, the Boers thought otherwise. To them war seemed inevitable, and they believe that the man who strikes first strikes best.

That the war presented many difficulties to our opponents cannot be denied. They were unexpectedly brought to a crisis, and were but half prepared to meet it. Their reinforcements were delayed in being transported thousands of miles. Their own subjects rose in rebellion and assisted the Boers. They were at first unacquainted with the country in which they had to fight.

How the enemy confronted and overcame these difficulties, and how their disadvantages gradually vanished like smoke, is well known. Troops, more troops, and still more were despatched to South Africa, until finally the Republics were literally flooded by the gentlemen in khaki. By the end of February, 1900, Lord Roberts had at his disposal tens of thousands, by whom General Cronje was surrounded and captured, and who paved the Field-Marshal's way for him to Bloemfontein and Pretoria. The difficulty and disadvantage arising from their not knowing the geographical features of the country in which they had to operate was gradually solved and cleared. Cape colonials enlisted in the British ranks, and these acted as guides and scouts. They knew the features of the country as well as the Boers, and could thus render very efficient service to the British. Still later, services of inestimable value were rendered to the British forces by natives, and, alas! even republicans themselves, who joined the enemy's ranks. When these enlisted, the English were provided with the best of guides, scouts and spies.

The disadvantages of the enemy were, to a large extent, the advantages of the, Boers. They had a very accurate knowledge of the country where they were fighting. The value of such a knowledge can hardly be over-estimated. If they had not known the country as well as they did, the English forces would certainly have been more successful in effecting their capture; and they would have often been in a sad plight. Our knowledge of the field of operations proved our salvation on more than one occasion, and was at the bottom of some successes achieved over the enemy. To know every mountain, hill, river, brooklet, valley, or donga is to be forearmed. The general that knows the battlefield is infinitely better off than the one that does not. He knows precisely how and when to lead an attack, or what to do when unexpectedly attacked. Now the Boer commanders had this intimate knowledge of the country, a knowledge which served them in good stead, and accounts for the Boers' marvellous mobility. They were not tied to roads, but could move in any direction, by night as well as by day, without ever losing their track. This the enemy could not do, not even with the aid of scientific instruments. When the natives and some of the burghers attached themselves to the British forces, then, and then only, were they able to make forced marches by night, and surprise the Boers when least expected.

A second point in favour of us was the fact that we were all mounted, whereas, at the commencement of the war, the British army consisted largely of infantry. The Boers are splendid horsemen—none more at home in the saddle than the farmer. The way he handled his steed, and the posture he assumed on it, invariably distinguished him, even at great distances, from the British soldier. The British infantry, however well they might have fought—and they did often fight bravely—were yet placed at a great disadvantage in engagements with the mounted Boers, who could quickly, sometimes too quickly, abandon untenable positions and occupy others which offered greater advantages.

Last, but not least, the Boers had the moral advantage of fighting in defence of their country. They did not fight for honour or glory, nor because of lust or greed for gold or expansion of territory, but for their beloved Fatherland, for that freedom which they had enjoyed so long and loved so well. This was their stimulus, their very inspiration to endure hardship and sacrifice all. What was the stimulus and inspiration of the British forces?

We shall now review some of the disadvantages under which we had to wage war for almost three years. No sooner had the war been declared than the Republics were almost completely isolated from the civilised world. The English were in possession of all the harbours, and if it had not been for Delagoa Bay, which is a neutral port, the communication of the Republics with the outer world would instantly have been cut off entirely. Through this port all contraband of war was strictly prohibited; and such foreigners as came to our assistance had to exercise great ingenuity to find their way *via* Delagoa Bay to the Boer lines. For several months in succession the Boers had to fight without the slightest encouragement from abroad. How the nations were regarding their struggle, whether any of them would dare to interfere on their behalf, and so indicate the rights of the weak against the strong—such and similar questions remained unanswered. Neither was the average Boer much concerned as to what other nations thought about the war. He was involved in the struggle, not because he courted it or loved to fight, but because his country was invaded and his independence was at stake. To secure his liberty he would resist any Power, regardless of all adverse criticism on the part of other Powers. Yet it proved no less a serious disadvantage to the Republics to have been so isolated, their communication with the other Powers so restricted, and themselves encompassed almost on every side by British dominions.

Not only was our intercourse with the outer world sadly impeded, but our internal communication was likewise seriously disturbed. The British, having divided the two states into several small sections by their blockhouse system, made it extremely difficult for the different commandoes to come in touch with one another. Our despatch riders, who had to beat their way through the various blockhouse lines, were sometimes so hemmed in by these that escape was impossible, and thus their despatches fell into the hands of the enemy. Towards the latter part of the war we were entirely dependent upon despatch riders for the transmission of our reports or messages. We had no more the inestimable advantage of heliographic instruments or telegraph wires, which were at the disposal of the British. Our reinforcements often arrived too late at the scene of action because the reports were delayed on the way, and so a battle was lost where a victory might have been secured.

The number of able-bodied men that the Republics could put in the field against the British forces was extremely limited. They had to contend against great numbers, and these numbers were reinforced from time to time. While the Boer numbers decreased, those of the enemy increased. It was certainly an heroic action on the part of two small republics to enter upon a contest with the British Empire, not to say with England, but was it not more heroic for these untrained farmers to confront and defy the overwhelming numbers brought against them? Surely this, if nothing else, should entitle the Boer to a place in the history of nations. Is this not proof sufficient that, when their Governments with their consent despatched an ultimatum, it was not arrogance which prompted them to take up arms against the British, but steadfast determination to vindicate their sacred rights at any price?

As to the numbers that were employed during the war, the official statement of the War Department makes the number of officers and soldiers that were engaged in active service in

South Africa about 500,000. To this must be added the number of armed natives, which would increase the sum total considerably. The Boer estimates vary, yet we do not hesitate to state that not more, but rather less, than 50,000 Boers were ever in the field. Of these a large proportion usually remained in the laagers, and never fired a shot at the enemy. After Prinsloo's surrender there were hardly 8,000 men still in the field. According to these numbers, the odds were ten to one. According to other authorities, the odds were even greater. One English writer says: "What glory shall a mighty empire win from a victory over 15,000 farmers? We are forcing upon our army the cruel humiliation of beating our enemy by sheer force of fifteen against one; we who used to boast that one Briton was a match for any three of his foes." The official returns at the close of the war substantiates the above figures, and show that it has not by any means been exaggerated. General De Wet, on being asked how long he thought the war would last if the numbers could be inverted, remarked: "As long as it would take to cable defeat to England." We do not wonder that some of the burghers eventually became discouraged and surrendered to the foe, especially when we think how great the odds were against which they had to contend month after month. We are rather surprised that so many did not become disheartened, but unflinchingly maintained the struggle until their Governments and leaders advised a general surrender.

Not only had we to confront such overpowering numbers, but these forces were under the control of England's most distinguished generals, men who combined practical experience with the advantage of a military training. These generals for the most part had achieved glory and renown in many a campaign—in Afghanistan, Egypt, and elsewhere—and thus came to South Africa, not to get their first lessons in warfare, but as experienced leaders of a great army. With such men to lead the British forces on to battle, if not to victory, three months were considered all too long by many to crush and wipe out of existence two small republics.

Opposed to these (famous) British officers stood the inexperienced Boer leaders. What a contrast! The Boer officers, with very few exceptions, were men without a shadow of military training, some even poorly developed mentally. They were, with few exceptions, peasants pure and simple, who left their ploughfields and flocks to take upon themselves the command over no less inexperienced burghers. These Boer leaders, elected by the people in times of peace, went to the front without the least practical knowledge of warfare. True, a few of them, such as Cronje, De la Rey, and Prinsloo had been leaders in Kaffir wars, and in such the burghers placed implicit confidence. Needless almost to state that in most of these so-called Kaffir warriors the Boers were utterly disappointed. It was one thing to attack natives badly armed, it was another thing to face an organised army well equipped with death-dealing instruments. We were thus at a great disadvantage at the commencement of hostilities as far as leaders were concerned. Gradually our staff of officers was improved, for the best men came to the front, and some of the older officers, who were unfit, were replaced by younger and abler ones. All these changes, however, took a long time, and were not effected before we had been subjected to two great disasters: one that of Cronje's capture on the 27th of February, 1900, the other, Prinsloo's surrender on the 1st of August, 1900, disasters which proved decisive epochs in the Anglo-Boer war.

Some of the Boer leaders, though inexperienced and untrained, proved themselves quite a match for their opponents. They have astonished military circles by their valorous actions and daring enterprises, and have merited imperishable honour and glory. Well may we be proud of leaders such as Louis Botha, Christian De Wet, and Jacobus

De la Rey, men whose names deserve a place in the rolls of history. We were fortunate in securing the services of such men at a time when they were most needed. No doubt it was to the advantage and not, as some maintain, to the disadvantage of the Free State burghers when C.R. De Wet was elected Hoofd Commandant at Brandfort in March, 1900. He, too, was but a farmer; culture he lacked, military training he had none, but the spark of martial genius had fallen and kindled in his breast. In figure, manner, and dress he was hardly distinguishable from hundreds of his country-men, who were not sharers of his military abilities. Does not his broad forehead indicate thoughtfulness? While his keen and penetrating eyes and firmly set lips are marks of determination and singleness of purpose. And his broad chin, does it not reveal the man of tenacity and endurance? As an individual he was sympathetic, generous, and magnanimous; he was endowed with discretion and tact, simplicity and honesty. As a soldier, vigilant, persevering, never indiscreet in anger or disappointment, but always courageous and resourceful. Recognizing the advantages of a surprise, he never lost an opportunity of harassing the enemy. Through his rare topographical knowledge of his country he baffled the foe by his movements time and again. Followed up by overwhelming numbers, he was compelled more often to evade fighting than offer battle. Never unduly elated, he was bravest and supreme when all others lost heart. He had to contend against treachery, desertion and want, but rose above all these obstacles, and proved himself the most powerful obstructor that the British columns had to encounter in South Africa. Such a man was a boon to his country, and to him the burghers confidently entrusted themselves and their interests. He has proved himself worthy of that trust. But all were not De Wets. There were, alas! Prinsloos, Vilonels, etc., too.

So much for the Boer officers. As regards our rank and file, they were as inexperienced in military matters as most of their leaders. The Boer is no soldier in the technical sense of the term. He was never subjected to military discipline, and unaccustomed to any restrictions. It took him months to realise the absolute necessity for and inestimable value of good discipline. The burghers looked upon themselves as volunteers, and such they really were. Now, when the enemy had to be attacked in their forts or strongholds, the Boer officers had to call out volunteers, as it was hazardous to lay too much pressure on the burghers to charge any position without their consent. To exercise too great power or authority over burghers was, at all times, especially at the beginning of the war, a risky thing. The officers knew well that the Boer is more easily led than driven.

Corps such as the Johannesburg and Swaziland Police and the Staats Artillery of the Transvaal and Orange Free State, which had the benefit of military training and discipline, proved their superiority over the rest of the burgher forces, and greatly distinguished themselves in the South African campaign. If all the burghers had had the same training as these corps, greater successes might have crowned their efforts during the early part of the war. The soldier, on the contrary, is no volunteer. His wishes are never consulted; when instructed to march on, he has to obey, though it may mean certain death to him, as was so often the case.

Another point of great disadvantage to the Boers is the lamentable fact that thousands of the surrendered and captured burghers enlisted in the British ranks as "National Scouts." This, viewed from the Boer standpoint, is the darkest spot in the South African campaign. Gladly would we dismiss this matter without any further comment, for it merits silent contempt, but we cannot help noting at what a terrible disadvantage we were placed by the action of these "National Scouts." As they made common cause with the enemy they furnished the latter from time to time with full particulars of our tactics, and divulged all our military secrets to the British. Moreover, they served the British forces as guides and led them forth at dead of night to surprise their countrymen in their secret, and otherwise unknown, retreats, where they were often captured or shot down by the enemy. Before these enlisted, night assaults by the English were out of the question. It was perfectly safe to bivouac some six miles from the enemy. For when the British did make a move during the night, they usually lost their way, as was the case when Gatacre undertook a night march on the Stormberg positions. With Boers as guides it was possible for the English forces to assume tactics hitherto untried by them.

Ah! brother, national scout, who may be reading this, do you not regret and lament the unhappy part of traitor? Are your hands not stained with the blood of your countrymen? And your conscience, is that not tarnished with the blood of men, women and children, who fell in Freedom's holy war? We do not despise but we pity you, and wish it were otherwise.

Not only did these "National Scouts" lead the British to the Boers, but they were the principal instruments in the hands of the enemy to clear the Republics of all foodstuffs and ammunition. They knew precisely where their fellow-burghers had stored away their meal, corn, fodder, and ammunition, knew where the oxen and sheep were grazing, and forthwith to these they conducted the enemy's forces, and thus was brought to pass that state of affairs which necessitated the Boers to lay down their arms. Without the assistance of the deserted burghers it would have taken the enemy ever so much longer to have exhausted the Republics entirely of all their resources. To a large extent these very republicans who sided with their country's enemies became the despoilers of the once so fair Republics. Ah me, that this should be recorded!

Besides, by assisting the enemy they not only encouraged them, but greatly discouraged their brethren in the field. The burgher who really meant well naturally became disheartened that those who fought with him for one and the same object could turn against him and play such a low and treacherous part. How men, who have stooped to deeds so mean and foul, shall defend their loathsome actions at the bar of Conscience and Justice, I know not.

In addition to the "National Scouts"—as though these were not more than sufficient—we had to contend against thousands of blacks, aboriginal natives armed by the British and taken up in their ranks. We naturally felt indignant at the adoption of coloured races in the British army; for we regarded it as an unwritten agreement between the respective Governments that no blacks were to be involved in the war. It was to be white *versus* white, Boer *versus* Briton. Hence, when the natives became embroiled in the struggle we refused to acknowledge and treat them as combatants. No quarter was given to armed natives that were not British subjects, and even these forfeited their lives on more than one occasion. This action, regarded superficially, may seem cruel and unjust, but remembering that war had not been declared against the natives, and also that, if we did treat them as English soldiers, we would simply have courted the opposition of all the natives, it does not seem quite so cruel and unjust. We had to resort to severe measures so as to let the natives fully realise that they were not acknowledged combatants, and thus could not claim the privileges of combatants. Surely the odds were already great enough—why then adopt blacks? We hold that the Military Government was not justified in the use of armed natives, and surely their adoption did not tend to the glory and honour of the British arms in South Africa.

Again, one must remember that for fully eighteen months we were entirely dependent upon the enemy for all military supplies. Our limited resources were soon exhausted, and, as the English controlled all the ports, the importation of arms, ammunition, horses, saddles, foodstuffs, and other necessaries, was out of the question.

The general opinion as to the duration of the war was that it would or could only last till the limited supply of Boer ammunition was spent. This limited supply, however, like the widow's oil, was not exhausted even after two years and eight months, and certainly never would as long as British factories provided rifles, ammunition, and other military equipments.

For eighteen months we were provided, directly or indirectly, by the British Government with the necessaries of war. Britain was supporting two armies in the field, armies which were not animated by a very friendly spirit toward each other. Our support, however, demanded at times the sacrifice of precious lives. When a commando ran short of ammunition a determined onslaught to secure more was planned, and often successfully carried out. The ammunition was obtained, but, alas! it cost them the blood of some of their bravest men. Such dependence was a great drawback to us. The Home Government also indirectly provided the fighting Boers with clothes. At first the burgher had his own private supply of clothing; but when the policy of destruction was resorted to his clothes were consumed by the flames, and he had to apply to the British Government for others. And this is how he did it. When he made a prisoner he would exchange clothes with him, provided better ones were thus secured, which was not always the case. With a certain amount of etiquette and dignity, this bargain was closed. Tommy, without any demonstration or remonstrance, would take off his jacket, pants and boots, and hand these to his brother Boer, with some such remark: "I don't grudge you it, sir—I know you fellows need them clothes badly; we have burnt yours, we shall get others again." "Out boots, out trousers, out jacket," were the abrupt commands of some of the Boers who had but little English.

To put an end to this process of exchanging outfits, Lord Kitchener issued a proclamation which forbade, under penalty of death, any fighting Boer to dress in khaki. This proclamation was not heeded, for the simple reason that men who had the interests of their country at heart were not likely to surrender because their clothes were wearing out. This threat but added one more to the many risks of death they ran. And so a few of these unfortunate burghers, captured in khaki dress because they had no other, were shot in accordance with the proclamation. This did not, however, intimidate the rest, for at the close of the war several hundreds were dressed in the dirty khaki hue.

In conclusion we note one point more, which counted seriously against the late Republics. It was this: the field of operations became more and more circumscribed and narrowed down by the extension of the blockhouses. The two Republics were divided, so to speak, into a great many little states by the blockhouse lines. The Free State alone was divided into at least eight or nine sections. Now these divisions, fenced round on every side, were cleared, one after the other, of all cattle, sheep, and other foodstuff. The British concentrated their forces in each section and operated there until it resembled a wilderness. And so they went from one division to another, until finally almost the whole country—both Transvaal and Free State—was denuded and in a semi-famine state. Owing to this confined and limited area in which we had to move, it was absolutely impossible for us to safeguard our war supplies.

Another result of this restricted area was the release of all prisoners-of-war taken by us. Thousands were captured, disarmed, and released to take up arms the next day. The same soldier has been captured two, three, and four times over. In this way it was impossible to reduce the forces of the enemy to any appreciable extent. The Boers certainly would have taken greater pains and dared more to capture the enemy's forces if they too had had a place of confinement; but no Ceylon or Bermudas were at their disposal. If they had had any such place, the Imperial Yeomanry and others would not have surrendered perhaps quite so readily. It certainly was a great misfortune to the late Republics that they could not retain their prisoners-of-war, while every Boer prisoner was either deported or guarded so securely, that, when once captured, he was entirely lost for the Boer cause. Under such unfavourable circumstances we had to fight our battle. It was against the stream all along. If ever there was an unequal contest, surely ours was one.

To show that we have by no means exaggerated the conditions in which we fought, we shall record here the resolution passed on the 31st of May, 1902, by the Volks Congress held at Vereeniging on the Vaal River, which reads as follows:—

"This meeting of Representatives of the people of the South African Republic and Orange Free State, held at Vereeniging, has learnt with regret of the proposal made by his Majesty's Government in regard to the cessation of existing hostilities, and of the intimation that this proposal must be accepted or rejected in an unaltered form."

> "The meeting regrets that his Majesty's Government has absolutely refused to negotiate with the Governments of the Republics upon the basis of our Independence, or to permit our Governments to enter into communication

with our Deputation."

"Our Peoples have, indeed, always thought that not only on the ground of Right, but also on the ground of the great material and personal sacrifices that they have made for their Independence, they have a just claim to such Independence."

"This meeting has earnestly taken into consideration the condition of land and people, and has more especially taken into account the following facts:—

"(1.) That the military tactics pursued by the British military authorities has led to the entire ruin of the territory of both Republics, with burning of farms and towns, destruction of all means of subsistence, and exhaustion of all sources necessary for the support of our families, for the maintenance of our forces in the field, and for the continuation of the war.

"(2.) That the placing of our captured families in the concentration camps has led to an unprecedented condition of suffering and disease, so that within a comparatively short time about 20,000 of those dear to us have perished there, and the horrible prospect has arisen that by continuing the war our entire race might be exterminated."

"(3.) That the Kaffir tribes within and without the borders of the territories of both Republics are almost all armed and take part in the struggle against us, and by perpetrating murders and committing all kinds of horrors, an impossible state of affairs has been brought about in many districts of both Republics, an instance of which took place lately in the district of Vryheid, where fifty-six burghers were murdered and mutilated in a shocking manner at the same time."

"(4.) That by Proclamation of the enemy, which he has already carried into effect, the burghers still in the field are threatened with loss of all their movable and immovable property, and so with total ruin.

"(5.) That through the circumstances of the war it has already long ago become impossible for us to retain the many thousands of prisoners-of-war taken by our forces, and that we thus could do but comparatively little damage to the British troops, whilst our burghers captured by the British are sent abroad; and that after the war has raged for nearly three years there remains only a small portion of the forces with which we entered into the war.

"(6.) That this remnant still in the field, which forms but a small minority of our entire people, has to contend against overwhelming odds, and, moreover, has reached a condition virtually amounting to famine and want of the necessary means of subsistence, and that notwithstanding our utmost endeavours and the sacrifice of all that we value and hold dear, we cannot reasonably expect a successful issue.

"This meeting is therefore of opinion that there is no reasonable ground for thinking that by continuance of the war our People will retain the possession of their Independence, and considers that under the circumstances the People are not justified in carrying on the war any longer, as that must tend to bring about the social and material destruction not only of ourselves, but also of our descendants.

"Urged by the above circumstances and motives, this meeting authorises both Governments to accept the proposal of his Majesty's Government, and on behalf of the People of both Republics to sign the same."

Such was the condition of the two Republics at the termination of the war. Well may one pause and ask: Has ever small nation, in similar circumstances, placed greater sacrifices, personal and material, on Liberty's shrine than the Republics? Have they not a lawful claim to that independence for which they fought so gallantly and so desperately, and for which they offered, ah! so much—their homes, their beloved families, their possessions and their lives?

Shall any still that stood afar off and watched the struggle, maybe sympathetically, or with cold indifference—shall they blame us for having surrendered? Verily not; for it cannot rationally be expected that a handful of farmers could offer resistance indefinitely, without any assistance, to a rich and mighty empire. The leaking vessel may ride to and fro for a while on the stormy billows, but eventually she is bound to sink; the shipwrecked mariner may struggle and swim, but, exhausted and powerless, he too goes down to find his last rest in the bosom of the deep. This was the case of the Republics. On the stormy billows of the ocean of war they were tossed hither and thither for nearly three years. Time and again they cried and signalled for relief, but no life-boats were sent to their rescue. None heeded their cry, or had compassion on them. The nations stood and looked on, sympathised and pitied, but did not help. And so, after all their strength was spent in trying to save the vessel of their independence, the gallant crew, with ship and all, sank beneath the waves of conquest.

CHAPTER IX

THE BOER AS SEEN IN THE LIGHT OF THE WAR

People tell
Of an old savage.

—Omar Khayyam

'E 'asn't got no papers of his own,
'E 'asn't got no medals nor rewards,
So we must certify the skill 'e's shown.

—Rudyard Kipling

It is with reluctance we approach a subject on which in past years so much has been written, often falsely. Besides, it is certainly a most delicate matter to expatiate on the character of any individual or nation.

We are aware that some of our readers will read the remarks on this subject—Boer character—with considerable suspicion and distrust. They may argue that the writers, being of Dutch extraction themselves, are not likely to give an accurate and dispassionate estimate of the character of their own people. They may even fear that our national sentiments might influence and predominate over our judgment, and switch us off the track of strict impartiality. If there be such, we can only assure them that we have no intention whatsoever of eulogising and extolling the race with which we are connected by blood.

In the past the Boers, *i.e.*, the Dutch element in the late Republics, have frequently been described, and as often maligned, by men who were perfect strangers to them; men who had not taken the least trouble to study their habits and character so as to arrive at a better understanding of the people they were trying to describe. Hence the various contradictory statements and representations of one and the same people. Alas! that they should ever have been the victims of so much cheap slander, that some men should have vied with one another in heaping insult and infamy on their heads, while others conjured up for themselves a fantastic and outrageous monster, and called that a Boer. We cannot expect that minds so inflamed and exasperated would do justice to the Boers. We feel convinced that their character can only be portrayed correctly and justly by men not animated by hostile sentiments towards them, but who, having been in touch with them have generously entered into their feelings and aspirations, and have looked at things from the Boer standpoint, as well as from their own; men who have had patience to bear with their infirmities; in a word, by men from their very midst—such and such only could do justice to their character.

Born and bred among the Dutch, associated with them all our lives, Dutch ourselves every inch—a fact in which we glory—our relations to the Boers, specially during the war, have afforded us excellent opportunities of making an ethnological study of them. During the war the Dutch population, more especially that portion of it which was directly connected with the struggle, passed through various phases and changes of life. Subjected to the most harassing circumstances, one saw them at their worst, but also at their best. Their virtues, as well as their vices, were fanned by the breath of war. Many a hidden virtue sparkled forth, as the dewdrop glistens in the beams of the rising sun. Many a slumbering vice and latent evil inclination found the regions of discord and strife a fruitful soil for development.

Now that hostilities have ceased, and the liberties of speech and the Press are extended once more, not only to such as were or are possessed of the bitterest of feelings towards the Dutch, but to all British subjects, we feel constrained to dissipate, if possible, some of the clouds of slander which encompassed the Boers before and during the war. Never in the history of nations has an honourable foe been more abused than the Boers. They have been misrepresented altogether to the world at large, and to the public in England in particular.

The war-Press, the platform, and even the pulpit, were all arrayed in martial order against them, and belched forth streams of abuse on two small states. A warm glow comes over our faces, and the blood begins to surge swiftly through our veins, as we recall some of the stinging expressions by which the Boers were stigmatised, and through which the mind of the English public was more and more inflamed, and all traces of sympathy with the Boers removed. We do not wish to enumerate these descriptive terms and phrases, for that would be raking up old scores. We would rather forget than remember unpleasant words and deeds.

We must, however, direct our attention briefly to the platform and pulpit, not to mention the Press, which were so successful in exercising an influence calculated to intensify race-hatred and obstruct the way to any peaceful settlement of political disputes.

When the Uitlanders in Johannesburg became dissatisfied with the existing state of affairs, and began to ask for greater privileges, they betook themselves to the platform. Now the Boers had no objection to their forming political organizations, or holding public meetings in which they could agitate for redress of grievances. But what they did object to, and very strongly, was the blatant manner in which these Uitlanders referred to their governments and themselves. Instead of exercising the art of "gentle persuasion" by laying their grievances before the Transvaal Government in the form of a polite request, and so achieving their desired object, these Uitlanders resorted to the policy of *fortiter in re*, the policy of intimidation, by threatening the Boers with the right arm of the British Empire unless they granted their requests instantly. When they adopted this method of procedure, they naturally did not get what they wanted. So they agitated and cried for redress of grievances until the unhappy war was brought about. Not only in South Africa, but also in England thousands were misled by these platform agitators, who were bent on placing the Dutch in a false light before the civilized world.

And the pulpit, as represented by some ministers not only of the Church of England, but also of the Nonconformist Churches, ministers of the gospel of peace on earth and good-will towards man—what an attitude did it assume! Surely if these clergymen had been as eager to promote peace as they were zealous to set in motion the waters of strife, they might, have accomplished a work meriting eternal reward. Alas! that some who are, or call themselves, followers of the Prince of Peace should have favoured a war of destruction, and been led to say very hard things and utter unfounded charges against the Dutch.

To cite only one of many instances, the Rev. Dr. Hertz, writing from Lourenco Marques, worded his letter thus:—

"We are safe, having left all we possess in the world behind us, and in all probability shall never see a single thing of it again. When I found the game the President and his crew were playing I thought it best to clear out ... The Boers have threatened to kill, burn, and destroy everything and everybody, *women* and *children*, and some of them at least are bad enough to do it. I had the verbal assurance of the President that I could stay safe and undisturbed, but he would not put anything in writing. Then they appointed a committee to give permits, and they would not give me one. And so it became more and more manifest that they meant to decoy me into staying, and then hold me at mercy. And what this mercy is may be seen from the last news from Johannesburg; any one without a written permit has been condemned to 25 lashes and three months' hard labour."

Such statements flowing from the pen of a Reverend Doctor were believed by thousands. Now what is the truth in regard to them? During the Bishop's absence his residence was specially guarded by order of the Government. The punishment meted out to some who remained in Johannesburg without permits exceeded in no case a higher fine than L3 *without* lashes. As to the Boers' intention of decoying the Doctor to stay, and then hold him at mercy, we need only remark that he must have thought more about his own importance than the Boers ever did. His assertion that the Boers threatened to kill everybody, including women and children, and that some of them are bad enough to do it, needs no refutation, for it merits silent contempt.

A feeling of sadness, if not pity, lays hold of one to think that ministers of the Gospel could actually draw up large petitions, urging the British Government to prosecute the war vigorously until the complete subjugation of the Boers was accomplished, which meant either their entire extermination or the sacrifice of their sacred rights.

There were, however, several notable exceptions, men who were not afraid to speak the truth about their enemies or their country's enemies, regardless of what others might think or say of themselves, regardless whether they would be called Boer-sympathisers or pro-Boers. Such men we shall ever revere and hold in estimation because they dared to speak the truth, cost what it would.

Thus far we have depicted the Boer character negatively in denying the unjust and unfounded charges brought against them by callous and misinformed minds. We do not hesitate to state that they are *not* a race of inferior beings, savage and uncivilized. They are not as good as some have presented them, they are not as bad as others have pictured them. Who, then, are these men and women who so stubbornly resisted British power and supremacy for such a long period under such great disadvantages? What are their main characteristics?

The Boers are the descendants of those pioneers who, for various reasons, left the Cape Colony between the years 1834-39. These emigrants or pioneers inspanned their large ox-waggons, bade farewell to their homes and farms in the Cape Colony and trekked across the Orange River. They traversed the wide plains of the late Orange Free State and proceeded to the Drakensberg Mountains. These mountains they crossed and settled down in Natal. How they were attacked and massacred by the Zulus, and how they, in their turn, defeated the Zulus and broke their power, how Natal became a British colony, all this is ancient history. The pioneers, objecting to English rule, quitted Natal. Some of them forded the Vaal River and they founded the Transvaal or South African Republic. Others settled west of the Drakensberg Range and founded the Orange Free State Republic.

These states were then infested by wild beasts and uncivilized native tribes. Against these the sturdy pioneers had to contend, and only after years of suffering, hardship, and bloodshed did they succeed, by their indomitable spirit, in vanquishing all foes, and so made habitable and opened up for commerce and civilization the Republics, which the late war has laid in ruins and ashes, indeed, converted into a howling wilderness, a land of desolation.

And these pioneers, whence came they, and what is their origin? They are descended from that race which so valiantly resisted and defied Spanish tyranny and power for eighty years, and so achieved that freedom of life, freedom of thought and freedom of belief, from which all Europe and England herself has derived priceless blessings. They are sprung from that stock whose courage was not shaken by the flames of funeral pyres, nor by all the tortures the human mind could devise; men who at the block betrayed no signs of fear, but faced death, as brave men ofttimes do, with a beatific smile, to the utter amazement of such as had to enact the cruel tragedy. These pioneers have in their veins the best blood of European nations, and their traditions are such as any nation might be proud of.

With such a history behind them, and descended from such ancestors, it is not strange that the most prominent feature in the Boer character is an intense and unconquerable love of freedom. His isolation, his large farm with outstretched plains or rugged mountains, and his manner of living, all tend to nourish that love of freedom in his bosom. Above all things he wants to be free and independent. His history is one long record of trekking away from British domination, not because he wishes to be exempted from all control and thus indulge in a lawless life, as some writers have erroneously maintained, but because he desires a government of his own. The chief desideratum with the Boer, in regard to government, is that it shall be his own, and not that of some other power, be it never so excellent a form of government.

When the Republics were annexed the English thought and hoped that the Boers would very soon take to the new Government, would be more than satisfied with the new arrangements, and so forget the privileges which they had enjoyed under the auspices of their own government. Those who thought and hoped thus were sadly disappointed. That powerful sentiment and that strong passion for freedom, seated deep down in the heart of the Boer, sustained them in bidding defiance to fearful odds for almost three years. That inborn passion enabled the Boer nation to sacrifice their all, and to endure for freedom's sake indescribable hardships and sufferings.

A Boer may not exactly know all that independence includes; he may not be able to enumerate the benefits accruing from it, but instinctively he covets it as a jewel of great price.

That this love of liberty and of country amounted to something more than mere sentiment has been proved conclusively by the war, when the whole male population rose in arms against the invading foe. Touching, indeed, it was to behold boys of twelve and grey-headed men of seventy and eighty years shouldering their rifles and all fighting for one great ideal. When their homes were burned, families removed, and goods taken or destroyed, they exclaimed: "Let the British do whatever they please, let them strip us of everything we hold dear, so long as we are only a *free* people. We do not mind being poor; we are prepared, when the war is over, to live in tents as our forefathers did; but we do not want to swear allegiance to the despoilers of our country. British subjects! *No, never.*"

And the Boer women, who are the very embodiment of

liberty itself, were they less enthusiastic and determined to be free than their husbands and sons? Verily not. Words fail us when we want to express our admiration for these heroines who played so prominent a part in the South African Campaign, and upon whom the brunt of the war fell. Alas! that this should have been the case.

In years gone by the wives and daughters of the early pioneers stood by the side of their husbands and fathers, casting bullets and loading their flint-lock guns, as the latter bravely repelled the fierce onslaught of Zulus, Matabeles, and other savage hordes. Many of them were ruthlessly murdered by these savage tribes. No Africander will ever forget names such as Weenen (Place of Weeping), Blood Rivier (Blood River), Vechtkop and Blauwkrants—places where Boer women had contributed their share of blood, that their children might be free. Those days were sad and dark; but there were sadder and darker times in store for the descendants of these pioneer women.

During the war the Republican women proved themselves no less formidable and brave than in those early days. When their husbands and sons were called to the front they took upon themselves the entire management of the farms. So well did they acquit themselves of such an onerous task that, as long as they were left unmolested, there was no lack of provisions for man or beast, always enough, and to spare. True, it cost them much labour and fatigue, for some of them had to tend the flocks, while others had to plough the fields and reap the crops in the scorching rays of a December or January sun. They did it willingly and gladly, so that the men might be free to engage in the struggle.

The enemy, on observing the attitude of the women, determined to strike a blow at them. They, so reasoned the enemy, had to be removed and gathered into concentration camps, if there ever was to come an end to the war. Not so much the men as the women were blamed for the prolongation of the war. The women first had to be subdued; the flames of freedom burning in their bosoms had to be extinguished. Hence the sad story of a war in which the weak and defenceless were made to suffer and endure so much.

When they were roughly handled and transported in ox-waggons, exposed for days to wind, sun, and rain, and were piled up in disease-stricken camps, did they flinch? When they and their children were dying in scores in these camps, did they beseech the burghers to relinquish the struggle, or petition the Boer Governments to yield? Verily not. On the contrary, in spite of their intense sufferings and of the appalling rate of mortality among them, they continually encouraged the burghers by sending out messages to them to this effect: "Fight on, don't yield; we would rather all die in the camp than see you surrender" "Go and fight," said one to her husband; "I would rather see you dead, and all my children dead, than that you burghers should cease the struggle." Another woman was so disappointed and disgusted at the surrender of her husband, that when he arrived at the concentration camp where she was confined she would have none of him, and quitted the camp the same night, making her escape to the Boer lines. Such women are the mothers of the next generation. Was it quite prudent on the part of the British to tempt them to rear their children in bitter hatred of the English race?

This liberty-loving feature in the Boer character has been beautifully described in the *Leek Times*:—

> "The old man, the youth and the stripling, are offering their hearts' blood as a sacrifice; nor do they think the sacrifice too great, strengthened and urged on by all they believe to be the highest and holiest in religion and

principle. The Boer will fight on, giving his last drop of blood and his last breath for his freedom. And the women-folk of his land are bearing their share of this task; they do not shrink; they are helping their fathers, brothers, and sons in this fight. They think no distance too great to travel, no burden too heavy to carry. The wife, with her little children round her knees, bids her husband a tearful but brave God-speed. The mother, as she gazes with a full heart on the boy who is as the apple of her eye, bids him go forth and fight in Freedom's Holy War. The lass bids her lover take his stand for all that she thinks worth having, esteeming him something less than a coward if he fails to the fight. Woe betide the oppressors when the women of a nation take up the quarrel."

Ah! thou mighty Christian England, who hast always prided thyself on being the most liberty-loving of all the Powers that be, how couldst thou have crushed the liberty of two small states? How couldst thou have torn so mercilessly the noble passions and aspirations of being free and independent from the Boer hearts? Hast thou verily extinguished by force the highest and holiest ambitions of a free-born people? Can the mountain torrent rushing down the valley be stemmed in its onward course? If patriotism is the ideal of a race that nourishes the most indestructible of all passions, then ye have indeed contended against an indestructible element of the Boer nature.

Next to and quite as prominent as this all-absorbing passion for freedom is the *religious trait* in the Boer character. As a people they are distinguished from all other nations by their religiosity. Remembering that they are the offshoot of men and women who perished in France, Holland, England and elsewhere for their faith, one does not wonder that they are religious. The religion of the Boer forms part and parcel of his very existence. His mind is imbued with the words and thoughts of Holy Writ. On a Sunday you will find him with his family, as a rule, attending service in his little chapel. If he cannot go to church, he will gather his family, increased sometimes by the presence of neighbours, round the family altar, and there he will read his Bible, sing his Psalms, bend his knees and lift up his heart in prayerful adoration to the God of his fathers.

Attaches, correspondents, and foreigners who fought on the side of the Boers were struck much by the simple piety, the religious ideas and sentiments of the Boers. Early in the morning and late at night their camps would resound with hymns. In this enlightened twentieth century, however, it has become the fashion to scoff and sneer at everything which savours of religion, so much so that it seems incredible to most that the Boers, as a people, can still be devout and God-fearing. Civilization with its concomitant vices has assumed the garb of Christianity, having its form and semblance, but missing its spirit and power. Such as are animated by the spirit of Christian religion and are endowed with its power are derisively called hypocrites. We shall willingly admit that there are many hypocrites among the Boers. But are they not found among all nations? To say that all religious Boers are hypocrites is utterly false.

When the English entered upon the contest with the Republics they evidently did not reckon with this religious factor of the Boer character. They did not know that the Boer would be supported as much by his religious sentiments as by his love of freedom to fight to the bitter end. Had they not been animated by such a fervent belief and childlike trust in Providence, they would have abandoned ere long a struggle which, regarded from a human standpoint, must have seemed hopeless to them. But they believed that their cause was a holy and just one, and that the God of Battles, the God of their forefathers, would ultimately crown their efforts and sacrifices by sending them a glorious deliverance. When the enemy desecrated their churches, ill-treated their pastors, and stabbed their flocks, cattle and horses, they were not disheartened, but said to themselves: "God in Heaven does behold, and He shall vindicate the cause of the just as well as that of defenceless creatures." Such deeds the religious Boer regarded with awe and aversion, and made him more determined than aught else not to surrender to those who perpetrated them.

The national anthems of the late Republics admirably express these two features of the Boer character. The following is a free translation of the Transvaal Volkslied, which may serve to illustrate the sentiments which have dominated the Boers ever since their national existence:

TRANSVAAL VOLKSLIED.

Right nobly gave Voortrekkers brave their blood, their lives, their all;
For Freedom's right, in Death's despite, they fought at duty's call.
Ho! Burghers, high our banner waves, the standard of the free,
No foreign yoke our land enslaves, here reigneth liberty.
'Tis heaven's command, here we should stand,
And aye defend the Volk and land.

What realm so fair, so richly fraught with treasures ever new;
Where Nature hath her wonder wrought, and freely spread to view!
Ho! Burghers old, be up and sing, God save the Volk and land,
Then, Burghers young, your anthem ring, o'er veldt, o'er hill, o'er strand.

And, Burghers all, stand ye or fall
For hearths and homes at country's call.

With wisdom, Lord, our rulers guide, and these Thy people bless,
May we with nations all abide in peace and righteousness.
To Thee, whose mighty arm did shield Thy Volk in bygone days—
To Thee alone we humbly yield all glory, honour, praise.
God guard our land, our own dear land,
Our children's home, their Fatherland.

A third distinctive mark in the Boer character, regarded from a military point of view, is his fearlessness, so strikingly displayed in several battles. That the Boers proved themselves brave during the war goes without saying.

Those who prophesied a speedy termination of the war in favour of the British thought that lyddite-shells and dum-dum bullets, when applied to the Boer, would at once scatter them far and wide, and so intimidate them that they would kneel and sue for mercy and peace. To their great disappointment they found the Boers stubbornly and gallantly resisting the most determined onslaught of the British forces, repelling them as often with disastrous results.

We admired, in friend or foe, no other quality more than bravery—bravery as distinguished from recklessness. We had respect for brave foes, and when the fortunes of war entrusted such as prisoners-of-war to our care, we always treated them with the courtesy gallant men deserve.

We often admired the valour displayed by our opponents. On certain occasions the British forces performed the most daring and heroic feats of which mortal men are capable. We saw officers and soldiers rushing and marching, as it were, into the very jaws of death. Though exposed to a storm of bullets, which consumed them like a withering fire, they would press on, often dropping down as wheat before the scythe. Such determination and bravery called forth the admiration of our men. There is, however, a difference between valour as displayed by the British and valour as displayed by the Boers. Without wishing to rob the British officer and soldier of their martial honours, which they may well deserve, having earned them at so great a cost, yet, in comparing Boer and Briton, we must bear in mind that the Boer had had no military training whatsoever, and was never subjected to military discipline. He hardly knew the importance and necessity of obeying orders promptly and implicitly. When he attacked or charged the enemy's stronghold or positions he did so, as a rule, of his own accord, not under any compulsion, but spontaneously and voluntarily. The British soldier, on the other hand, had all the advantages and sometimes disadvantages of military discipline. He had been taught to obey orders, whether it meant death to him or not. Besides, the soldier was backed up by thousands and tens of thousands of comrades on every side, while batteries of naval guns and Armstrongs were at his rear, under cover of which he could charge or retreat. No beating of drums, or symphonies of martial music, or great numbers inspired and urged the Boer on to the performance of heroic deeds. With rifle in hand and limited supply of cartridges he often had to face overwhelming odds. And when these odds threatened to outflank him, he was called by some a coward for retreating and not allowing himself to be captured. Instinctively he knew it was better to retreat—

> "For he who fights and runs away
> May live to fight another day."

Some maintain that the Boers are only brave when lying behind huge boulders, or entrenched in strong fortifications, from whence, concealed, they can pour a deadly fusillade on the approaching enemy. There may be an element of truth in this charge, but as a generalization it is utterly false. To stamp the Boers as cowards in general is to rob the British Army of much of its honour and so discredit their work in South Africa. The best answer to and the most persuasive argument against this assertion is to be found in the construction of the multitudinous forts, trenches, sangars, blockhouses, etc., by the British in South Africa. What is their significance? The most inobservant traveller in South Africa must be struck by the network of fortifications erected almost throughout the length and breadth of the country. Could the English have given the Boers a better testimonial of gallant behaviour than these? Surely blockhouses and bulwarks are not required for cowards, for they would never approach them.

It is hardly necessary to say that all Boers were not brave; there were many timorous ones among them. No army in the world is composed entirely of brave and fearless characters. We often sustained losses and sometimes disasters because the burghers retreated when they should have stood or charged. The victory would have often been theirs had they resisted a little longer. But apart from this, have they not proved to the enemy in particular and to the world in general that they are the children of chivalrous nations, of men who knew no fear? Have not the British forces sustained some of their greatest losses when these untrained peasants led the charge? We need only refer to a few of the many battles fought during the war to show what these simple untrained farmers did accomplish—battles which certainly merited for them the attribute of being brave.

(1) On the 30th of November, 1899, General De Wet, who was then only Assistant Commandant, led 200 men up Nicholson's Nek, a hill which was then in the possession of

the enemy. After an engagement which lasted five hours, the British hoisted the white flag. General De Wet personally counted 817 prisoners-of-war, while 203 were lying on the battlefield either dead or wounded. Here the English were in possession of the hill, *i.e.*, of the best positions, and vastly outnumbered the Boers.

(2) In the great battle of Spion Kop, which lasted eight days, the Boers were placed under the most terrific bombardment, and were constantly attacked by large numbers of the enemy—yet they warded off these attacks gallantly. On the night of the 23rd of January the English under cover of darkness scaled the mountain—Spion Kop—and were thus in possession of the key to Ladysmith. It was evident to the Boer generals that Ladysmith would be relieved if Spion Kop was not retaken. As soon as it became light the mountain was stormed from different directions by the Boers, who were determined, if possible, to wrench it from the grasp of the British. Both parties displayed amazing bravery. Boer and Briton fell side by side, staining the grass with their blood, and bespattering the stones and rocks with their brains. At dusk more than half of the mountain was in possession of the Boers. During the night the English evacuated it, and once more the Boers commanded over the entire mountain. It cost them 35 killed and 170 wounded, but their objective was achieved. Again the *British* were in command of the mountain, and were continually reinforced. After Spion Kop was retaken, no more white flags were hoisted by the Boers. On the contrary they lamented the loss of so many precious, innocent lives. The Rev. R. Collins, a chaplain with General Warren's Brigade, made the following statement *re* the attitude of the Boers after the battle:—

> "I venture to think it a matter of considerable importance to draw attention to the attitude of the Boers whom we met during the carrying out of our duties on these three

days. For my part I confess that the deepest impression has been made on me by these conversations, and by the manly bearing and straightforward outspoken way in which we were met.

"There were two things which I particularly noted. As there was no effort made to impress us by what was said (they spoke with transparent honesty and natural simplicity, and in nearly all cases the conversations were begun by us), so there was a total absence of anything like exultation over what they must consider a military success. Not a word, not a look, not a gesture or sign, that could by the most sensitive of persons be construed as a display of their superiority.

"Far from exultation there was a *sadness*, almost anguish, in the way in which they referred to our fallen soldiers. I can best convey the truth of this statement, and show that there is no attempt at exaggeration in using the word anguish, by repeating expressions used, not once, but again and again by great numbers as they inspected the ghastly piles of our dead—'My God! what a sight!' 'I wish politicians could see their handiwork,' 'What can God in Heaven think of this sight?'"

By such a spirit was the Boer animated when he achieved some of his most brilliant successes. He did not fight for honour and glory. He fought at duty's call as a patriot in a great cause.

(3) A few weeks prior to the battle of Spion Kop the Boers made their famous, though unsuccessful, attack on Platrand, known as Waggon Hill to the English, a hill situated three miles south of Ladysmith. This hill was occupied by the British, and formed as it were the key to Ladysmith. For it was practically impossible to bring about the fall of

Ladysmith so long as the British were on Platrand. A council of war accordingly decided to attack the enemy on the hill on the night of the 5th of January, and, if possible, expel them from it.

The Rev. J.D. Kestell, who accompanied the Boer forces, gives the following striking description of the attack—a description which conveys to the mind of the reader something of the awfulness of war, as well as of the courage and heroism displayed by Boer and Briton alike:—

> "On the summit the hill is level, and round about its crest runs a cornice, to use an architectural term, of great rocks, which we call a krantz in the Africander language. The British forts were built immediately above this krantz.
>
> "At about 10 P.M. we left the laager in order to climb the hill at half-past 2 A.M. Having reached Neutral Hill, we left our horses there and proceeded on foot. It was very dark, and all was still as death. We walked forward slowly and spoke only in whispers, and yet our progress was not so silent but that we feared we should be heard. In the silence of the night the slightest rustle of tree or shrub sounded loud in our ears, and the thud of our feet on the loose stones seemed to me like the tramp of a troop of horses. The enemy, thought I, would certainly become aware of our approach long before we could even begin to climb the hill. But it seems after all that I was mistaken, and that the sentry did not discover us until we had approached very close. At three o'clock we reached the deep dongas at the foot of the hill, and the foremost men passed through. In about twenty minutes we had climbed almost two-thirds of the hill, when we heard a beautiful voice ringing out in the morning air: 'Halt! Who goes there?'

"No answer came from us. We continued climbing. A moment passed, and then the silence was broken by a crash of a volley. Then another and another. Everywhere, above and in front of us, the flashes of the rifles leapt forth into the darkness, and the sharp reports followed in such quick succession as to give the impression of Maxims firing. All of a sudden I saw a great jet of flame, and instantly the thunder of a cannon broke upon the startled air, and presently behind us I could hear the shrapnel bullets falling on the ground.

"Then many of those who had not yet begun to climb the hill turned and fled; but others rushed upwards, and rapidly approached the cornice of rocks, whence the heavy firing issued. Silence was now unnecessary, and everywhere voices were heard encouraging the men.

"At half-past three we reached the reef of rocks and boulders, and presently I heard that two burghers had already been wounded, while another lay motionless, but it was as yet too dark to see who it was.

"Before long it became light, and some of the burghers charged the forts that were just above the ledge of rocks. They overpowered the soldiers there, and took them prisoners, but were forced to fall back to the escarpment of rocks immediately, on account of the heavy fire directed on them from the other forts. And now the roar of the cannons and rifles became terrific. This was especially the case with the ceaseless rattle of small-arms. One could with difficulty distinguish separate reports. All sounded together like one continuous roar, and awoke an echo from the Neutral Hill that sounded like the surging of a mighty wind.

"We found ourselves under a cross cannon-fire. The shells

from one of our guns flew over our heads, and exploded just in front of us on the forts, so that we were often in danger of being struck by our own shells; and the projectiles of the English were hurled in an opposite direction on our cannon forts and on the burghers on Neutral Hill.

"Gradually we began to see in what a terrible position we were. How terrible the firing was! It never ceased for a moment; for if the burghers did not rush out from time to time, to assail the forts, the English charged us. This alternate charging was taking place every now and then, and it was during these attacks that the pick of our men fell. Whenever a sangar was charged, a destructive fire was directed on our men, and then some gallant fellows would always remain behind struck down.

"It was a fearful day—a day that no one who was there will ever forget. The heat, too, was unbearable. The sun shot down his piteous rays upon us, and the higher he rose the hotter it became. It was terrible to see the dead lying uncovered in the scorching rays; and our poor wounded suffered indescribable tortures from thirst. And there was nothing to give them—only a little whisky which I had got from an English officer, who had been taken prisoner. I gave a little of that—only a few drops—to every wounded man. Not only the wounded—all of us suffered from thirst. Long before midday there was not a drop of water left in our flasks. So intolerable was the thirst that there were burghers who went down to the dongas below in search of water, where there was none, and where they knew that almost certain death awaited them.

"How slowly, too, the time dragged on! 'What o'clock is it?' someone asked. It was then only ten o'clock, and it seemed as if we had been fighting more than a day, for up to that moment the firing had continued unabated.

"Twelve o'clock passed, one o'clock, two o'clock—and still the fire was kept up; and still the burning rays of the sun were scorching us. Clouds! But they threw no shadow over us. Everywhere small patches of shadow chequered the hills and valleys, but they seemed to avoid us. But a black mass of cloud is rising in the west, and we know that everything will soon be wrapped in shadow. Nearer and nearer to the zenith the clouds are rising. What is that deep rumbling in the distance? Thunder! Nearer and nearer it sounds, and presently we hear it overhead above the din of the musketry and the boom of the cannon. How insignificant the crash of the cannons sounds now. It is as the crackle of fireworks when compared with the mighty voice of God!

"We got more than shadow from the clouds. At five o'clock great drops splash on the rocks. Presently the rain fell in torrents, and I could wash the blood of the wounded from my hands in it.

"It was now just when the rain was descending in sheets of water, and the thunder-claps were shaking the hills, that the enemy redoubled their efforts to drive us off the ledge, and our men had to do their utmost to repel the determined onslaught. Had they been driven down the hill, every burgher fleeing for his life would have formed a target for the enemy. The fight was now fiercer than at any time during the day. It was fearful to hear the roar of the thunder above and the crash of the rifles below. But the enemy did not succeed in driving us off. We remained there two and a half hours longer. Meanwhile we had been able to quench our thirst. Streams of water dashed down through the rocks, and we drank our fill. These streams of water came from the forts a few yards above us, and were red in colour. Was it red earth, or was it the blood of friend or foe that coloured the water? Whatever the cause, we were so thirsty that nothing would have kept us from drinking. After the English had done their utmost to drive us from the hill, and been baffled in their attempts, they returned to their forts, and the firing subsided for a short time.

"At last the sun set, and at half-past seven we withdrew. We had been on the hill for sixteen hours, under a most severe fire, and now we retired; but we were not driven off by the Devons with levelled bayonets, as I have read in an English book. We were not driven off the hill. We held it as long as it was light, and when twilight fell and no reinforcements came, we considered it useless to remain there. Including the Transvaalers we had lost 68 killed and 135 wounded."

(4) One instance more to show that the Boers behaved gallantly not only under cover or when scaling mountains or hills occupied by the enemy, but also when they met the foe on the plain without any cover at all.

Lord Methuen's column, 1,500 strong, was charged in broad daylight on the open veldt by about 700 burghers. The whole convoy with four Armstrong guns was captured. Besides this the enemy lost 400 in killed and wounded, and 859 prisoners of war, including Lord Methuen himself, who was wounded in the leg. The Boer casualties amounted to 9 killed and 25 wounded. Do not such engagements prove that the Boers could hold their own not only behind stones and in trenches but also on the plain?

Lord Methuen's column was not the only one which was attacked and taken on the exposed veldt. Some of the most brilliant achievements of the Boers were accomplished when they were altogether exposed to the enemy's fire and had to take the offensive. Was it then arrogance and vainglory which prompted them to offer battle to one of the great Powers of the world? Arrogance and vainglory would not have stood the test, but would soon have vanquished like morning clouds before the rising sun. There must have been some other cause. What was it?

Here, then, the reader has another reason why the Boers fought so long. As a people they are brave, and thus scorn the very thought of surrendering like cowards. They chose to die as *men*, and the memory of those who fell as such shall ever be dear and sacred to us.

> "For how can man die better
> Than facing fearful odds,
> For the ashes of his fathers
> And the temples of his gods?"

Another trait in the Boer character is his wonderful resourcefulness and his ability to cope with difficulties. It was as much this phase of his character as his patriotism, religiosity and valour which enabled him to continue the struggle so long. If the Boers had not been so wonderfully resourceful, and understood so well how to lighten their burdens and solve their problems, they never could have held out so long.

Surrounded on almost every side by British dominions, with all imports cut off, they were bound to fall back on their own limited resources. When these were exhausted, they had to plan some way out of the difficulty. And so ingeniously did they contrive to find the wherewithal for the prosecution of the war, and the necessaries of life, that it must have appeared hopeless to the enemy at times that the Republicans should ever be reduced to such an extremity that they could help themselves no longer.

And this is the way they planned. When their boots wore out, men were appointed to tan hides and make boots; even the women busied themselves in this kind of work. When there was a great scarcity of soap,—an article used also by Boers,—the women boiled a serviceable substance with the help of the ashes of various weeds. When the British began destroying the mills everywhere mills were mounted on waggons and carried off on the approach of the enemy. When tobacco failed the burghers, Nature made provision once more. Leaves of different kinds of trees were taken, dried and soaked in a weak solution of tobacco extract, and when dry these leaves answered the purpose of tobacco. The fine handicraft of great-grandmothers in the spinning of wool was revived. The women-folk, constructing spinning-wheels from old sewing-machines, spun wool beautifully, and knitted socks and other articles as fine and as strong as any that can be bought in shops. When the English took or burnt all their vehicles they reconstructed others from the remnants of the burnt ones. One woman was seen with a cart in which two plough wheels were placed. It looked strange, but answered the purpose well enough. When salt was not to be had for love or money, wells were dug in the pans and salt water was found, from which, by a process of evaporation, salt was obtained. In this manner one problem after the other was solved. As to their clothes, overcoats were made of sheep-skins, and some burghers wore complete suits made of leather. The worn-out clothes were patched with soft leather and then they were said to be "armoured." Besides this there was the "shaking out" process, as it was called by the burghers. The Boers thought that they were quite justified in exchanging clothes with Tommy Atkins whenever he was captured; for the English had destroyed and burnt theirs as often as they could. As we had no means of import, and as the enemy had burnt our clothes, who shall condemn our action, however humiliating it might have been to the soldier or costly to the British Government to provide outfits for both parties? Necessity knows no laws. In the same way the burghers were provided with rifles, ammunition, horses, saddles, bridles and other necessaries by the British. When their ammunition first ran short, many were not a little concerned about it, and thought that that would ultimately compel them to surrender. But the English were kind enough to supply them, so that after each fight, as a rule, they had enough to commence another with. Towards the latter part of the war the English were fought and often beaten with their own arms. So, as far as that was concerned, the Republics could have prolonged the war indefinitely, or at least as long as they were being supplied by the British Government. Does this often happen in the history of wars—a foe lashed by its own weapons?

In his social intercourse the Boer is kind-hearted, tender and hospitable. He loves to be kind—to be hard and cruel is contrary to his nature. Owing to his soft and gentle disposition he sometimes brought disaster and ruin upon himself during the war. Traitors and renegades were mercifully spared, and these notorious beings were instrumental in bringing about his defeat. In times of peace kind-heartedness no doubt is a virtue of intrinsic worth; in times of war it cannot always be exercised.

In outward appearance the Boer may be, and sometimes is, somewhat stern and uncompromising; but those who have gained his confidence and known him best have invariably discovered behind and at the bottom of this seemingly forbidding exterior a softness of disposition and a tenderness of heart which brooks no rivalry. Men who have taken the Boer character second-hand, or have not taken the trouble to enter into his feelings or obtain his friendship, have often been misled by his quiet phlegmatic demeanour, which at times verges on stolidity. They have described him as being sour, morose and unkind. To such he appeared a sort of obstreperous, cantankerous being, who simply delights to quarrel with every man he meets—especially if an Englishman came in his way. Needless to say he is nothing of the sort.

During the war we were several times struck by the gentle nature of the Boers. They are indeed not that blood-thirsty, war-loving race which some have imagined them to be. We make bold to say that there is nothing which they so much dislike and abhor as shedding blood and inflicting torture and misery on humanity. They are essentially a peace-loving race, and will never indulge in war unless compelled by circumstances over which they have no control.

The British officers and soldiers who fell into their hands during the war can bear evidence from personal experience that the average Boer is dominated by kind and gentle sentiments. He treated the wounded soldier and the prisoner-of-war with kindness. He would share his last drop of water with the wounded, bandage his wounds to the best of his ability, and would extend to him all the medical attendance at his command.

Major J.B. Seely, Conservative M.P. for the Isle of Wight, who served with the Hampshire Yeomanry for many months in the Transvaal, confirmed the above statements in a letter to the *Times* in the following way:—

> "During the seventeen months that I have served in South Africa I had, perhaps, rather exceptional opportunities of learning how our wounded were treated by the Boers. On two different occasions men under my command who were dangerously wounded were attended with the greatest kindness and care by the Boers; and the wounded men

themselves begged me to thank those who had been so good to them. On both occasions the general in command of the column conveyed his thanks either personally or by letter. I have spoken to many officers and men who have been left sick or wounded in the hands of the Boers, and in no single instance have I heard anything but gratitude expressed for the treatment they had received. In the intense excitement of hand-to-hand fighting it may be difficult to differentiate between the wounded and unwounded, but the relatives and friends of those now fighting may rest assured that English left wounded on the field will receive from the Boers no less care and kindness than wounded Boers have invariably received from the English."

Such is the testimony of men who came in contact with the Boers at a time when one would expect that the demoralizing and hardening influences of war had removed every vestige of gentleness.

We never heard the Boers use strong and abusive language towards prisoners-of-war. On the contrary they would converse with them in a most genial and friendly spirit; so much so, that the onlooker could scarcely distinguish between Boer and Briton, friend or foe. Now when the Boers behaved thus towards their prisoners-of-war they only did what they ought to have done. When a man is captured or wounded he is no more an enemy in the literal sense of the word, and should not be treated as such. Military precautions must necessarily be taken to prevent the escape of prisoners, but, apart from that, men forced to surrender should neither be regarded nor treated as criminals, but as an honourable foe deserves. In making these remarks we do not infer that our wounded were not well attended to by the enemy. In most cases we believe they were. We shall not comment on the treatment extended to our prisoners-of-war. In the latter stage of the war we believe there was room for improvement, especially when natives were taken up in the British ranks. These natives treated our men shamefully at times, and went even so far as to commit the most brutal murders.

Not only did the burghers treat their prisoners-of-war well, but the Boer officers under whose immediate control they were placed dealt, as a rule, very kindly and leniently with them. Some of the more prominent Boer officers, such as General De Wet and others, have been accused occasionally of having ill-treated prisoners-of-war. Most of these charges on examination proved groundless.

Mr. Erskine Childers, in a letter to the *Times*, expressed himself on this matter as follows:—

> "It is time that a word was spoken in opposition to the idea that General C. De Wet is a man of brutal and dishonourable character. Those who, like myself, have served in South Africa, fought against him, and frequently met men who have been prisoners under him, look, I believe, with shame and indignation on the attempts made to advertise and magnify such incidents as the alleged flogging and shooting of peace envoys, so as to blacken the character of a man who, throughout the war, held a reputation with our troops in the field of being not only a gallant soldier, but a humane and honourable gentleman. We may deplore the desperate tenacity of his resistance. Our duty is to overcome it by smashing him in the field. We gain nothing but only lose our self-respect by slandering him.
>
> "His whole career gives the lie to such aspersions. It was in May of last year, ten months ago, that he first gained prominence. Since then he has fought scores of engagements with us, some successful, some unsuccessful, never

with a suspicion of dishonourable conduct. He has had at one time or another some thousands of our men in his hands as prisoners-of-war. Many of them I have myself met. At second or third hand I have heard of the experiences of many others. I have never heard a word against him. When men suffered hardships they always agreed that they could not have been helped. But, on the other hand, I have heard many stories showing exceptional personal kindness in him over and above the reasonable degree of humanity which is expected in the treatment of prisoners-of-war.

"I believe this view of him is universal among our troops in South Africa. It makes my blood boil to hear such a man called a brigand and a brute by civilian writers at home, who take as a text the reports of these solitary incidents, incomplete and one-sided as they are, and ignore—if, indeed, they know of it—the mass of testimony in his favour."

This testimony about De Wet, as well as other Boer officers, has been substantiated by scores of letters from other officers and privates.

The relation of the Boers to the coloured races in South Africa, and the treatment of the latter, have been a cause of much offence and misunderstanding. It is generally, though mistakenly, held that the Boers ill-treated the natives, and that in the most brutal and tyrannical manner. Such unwarranted assertions had furnished one of the various flimsy excuses for war in South Africa. The natives had to be protected! They were slaves, and must be liberated. Therefore—war! That natives have sometimes received bad treatment at the hands of their masters we shall candidly admit. In such instances the law-courts of the country stood open to them, where justice was at all times meted out to the guilty party.

On the whole, we maintain that the treatment of inferior races by the Boers contrasts very favourably with that by the British. The Dutch have always expressed themselves very strongly against the policy of placing the natives on a footing of political equality with the whites, because morally, intellectually, and industrially they are decidedly their inferiors.

Those who, like the American Bishop Hartzell, argued that the British cause ought to win, since the Boers do not equal the English in just treatment of inferior races, would do well to consider the following facts:—

(1) In the strip of East African coast—a British Protectorate—which faces Zanzibar *the full legal status of slavery* is maintained, and fugitive slaves have even been handed back to their owners by British officials.

(2) In Zanzibar and Pemba the manumission of slaves presided over by Sir Arthur Hardinge is proceeding slowly, and many thousands are still in bondage.

(3) In Natal the *corvee* system prevails, and all natives not employed by whites may be impressed to labour for six months on the roads.

(4) In Bechuanaland, after a rebellion some years ago, natives were parcelled out among the Cape farmers and indentured to them as virtual slaves for a term of five years.

(5) Under the Chartered Company in Rhodesia the chiefs are required, under compulsion, to furnish batches of young natives to work in the mines; and the ingenious plan of taxing the Kaffir in money rather than in kind has been

adopted, so that he may be forced to earn the pittance which the prospectors are willing to pay him.

(6) In Kimberley what is known as the compound system prevails. All natives who work in the diamond mines are required to "reside" under lock and key, day and night, in certain compounds, which resemble spacious prisons. So stringent is the system that even the sick are treated within the prison yard. On no pretext whatever is a native allowed to leave his compound.

During these months of incarceration the natives are separated from their women-folk and families. The consequence is one of the most striking and shocking features of the compound system. A number of the lowest, drink-besotted, coloured prostitutes, estimated at about 5,000, have collected at Beaconsfield, where, so to speak, they constitute a colony, occupying a revolting quarter of the township. When the natives come out for a short spell these unhappy women receive them. It is, no doubt, convenient from the standpoint of the company to have them there, for it probably prevents the natives from going away. This moral cancer is one of the direct and inevitable outcomes and concomitants of the compound system.

(7) The South African Dutch contribute more money annually to native mission work than the South African English. The English missions in South Africa are supported chiefly by funds from England. The largest and most handsome churches for natives in South Africa are those built by the Dutch. The Dutch Reformed Church in South Africa has more representatives in the foreign mission field than all the other English denominations in South Africa together.

If necessary, more facts bearing on this subject of native treatment could be adduced. One could, for example, point out how the aboriginal Tasmanians and Australians have been almost completely extirpated; how, in the name of civilization, thousands of Dervishes have been mowed down in Egypt, and how South African soil itself has been stained from time to time by the blood of Zulus, Basutos, Matabeles and other coloured races, who became the victims of British, and *not Boer*, arms. Remembering all this and much more, we claim that England has no right to cast the first stone at the Boer in regard to the treatment of coloured races.

The Boer's nature does not admit of such tyrannical actions of which he has constantly been accused. His native servants are treated almost as members of his own family, and often serve him voluntarily for several years in succession.

Mr. Chamberlain in a Parliamentary Debate has expressed himself on this matter as follows:—

> "Members of Parliament appear to be under the impression that the Boers in the Transvaal were fierce and unjust aggressors, and that they dispossessed the natives of their territory and brutally ill-treated them afterwards. I wish honourable members would read the papers before they came to this rash and inconsiderate conclusion. The absolute reverse of that was the fact."

The Boers, as a people and as individuals, are thoroughly hospitable, indeed we do not hesitate to affirm that no nation is more hospitable. To meet them, dwell in their midst, associate with them and know them, is to like, if not to love them.

The respectable traveller that lights on a Boer farm will invariably receive a cordial welcome. The farmer will politely invite him to his house, and will try to make his guest feel quite at home. Should it be late in the day, the guest will be expected to stay the night. A plain but substantial supper will fall to his share. The best bedroom and most comfortable bed will be at his disposal for the night, while his horses will receive every attention. In the morning he will be invited to breakfast before setting out on his day's journey. Should the traveller, on leaving, offer to pay the farmer for the night's accommodation, the latter will, as a rule, decline to accept any payment, nay, will regard it rather as an insult to be offered payment for his hospitality. Callous and unappreciative characters have abused such hospitality, and construed it as a mark of ignorance on the part of the Boer. He is, so they say, hospitable and ready to entertain *because* he is so stupid and ignorant. There may be a grain of truth in this assertion, but to attribute Boer hospitality exclusively to this is as false as it is mean.

> "... I never want to meet kinder, more hospitable, and more comfortable people than the Boers. True, some of them are poor and ignorant, but the general run of them live comfortably, rear their families well and with fair education. They are the reverse of what we have been taught to consider them. It will be a happy day for Australia when our pastoral country is settled by as fine a class of people."

Thus wrote a Queensland officer, Major Spencer Browne, while Mr. R.H. Davis, an Englishman who had resided for some time in Pretoria, offers the following testimony:—

> "I left Pretoria with every reason for regret. I had come to it a stranger, and had found friends among men whom I had learned to like for themselves and for their cause. I had come prejudiced against them, believing them to be all the English Press and my English friends had painted them—semi-barbarous, uncouth, money-loving, and treacherous in warfare. I found them simple to the limit of

their own disadvantage, magnanimous to their enemies, independent and kindly."

The trait that we admire and cherish most in the Boer character is their hospitality. We shall ever gratefully remember how kindly our burghers were received by many a colonial farmer, such as the Van der Merwes of Toutelboschkoek and Bamuur, Calvinia district, the Therons of Rietpoort, Richmond, the two Miss Van der Merwes of Badsfontein, Murraysburg, and a host of others whose names we cannot mention here, as well as non-combatant farmers of the late Republics. Weary and worn out by the fierce and unequal contest we were often refreshed at their tables, and were so invigorated by their kindness and hospitality that, after a brief respite, we could once more resume the struggle with fresh determination and revived energies.

Never shall we forget the kindness shown to us personally during the years of strife. And here we would express our sincere thanks to all such as alleviated so greatly the burdens war had imposed upon us—alleviated these by friendly sympathies, which found expression in deeds of kindness and love, and that at a time and in circumstances when the sword of Damocles was suspended over their heads, for to give an enemy a drop of cold water was then considered a great crime!

The Boers are *passionately fond* of their homes and families. The little cottage, with the garden, the flocks and herds—in these they take pleasure. To accumulate and hoard up wealth is not their sole ambition or ideal of life. If they possess enough to live comfortably, give their children a fair education and meet their bills, they are content.

Now this passionate devotion to their homes and families, however commendable a virtue it may be, proved most detrimental to their best interests when the waters of strife were set in commotion. Nothing was so trying to the Boers than to be separated from their families for months and months. Up to the commencement of the war the Boer farmer hardly knew what it meant to be away from his family for a long time. Owing to this strong attachment to, one might almost say weakness for, their homes, the burghers often insisted on obtaining leave of absence to visit their families, and that at times when their services were most needed on the battlefield.

This love of home and property must account for a great number of voluntary surrenders to the British. When the enemy entered the Republics the farmers had to choose between surrender or sacrificing hearth and home, property and all they had—entrusting these to the mercy of the foe. Many, be it said to their honour, deliberately chose to sacrifice all rather than their independence. Others lay down arms, to protect or save, as they thought, their families, homes and property. Sadly and bitterly were they disappointed; for their homes were still burned, and their families confined in the concentration camps.

These, then, are some of the more striking features of the Boer character. To summarize them in one sentence: the Boer loves his Country and Freedom, his Bible and Rifle, his Neighbour and Family.

Are these not qualities which recommend themselves as worthy of admiration? Are they not indications of much that is noble and good, even though the foe be vanquished? Do not the English pride themselves in possessing these very qualities, qualities which, they say, have made them a great and mighty nation? Be it so; let them gently deal with the Boer, who is possessed of these noble attributes in common with themselves. We hope that they will treat their new subjects with due consideration. What a happy day will it be for South Africa when Boer and Briton, through the length and breadth of that blood-stained land, have learned the secret of living as friends and brothers, respecting one another, as befits Christian people. Will that happy day ever dawn, or is South Africa doomed to be a land of discord? Let us hope that the unhappy past will gradually be effaced from the memory of both Dutch and English. Let the English Government exercise discretion in introducing a South African policy which shall tend to reconcile and unite, not embitter and sever.

What about the faults and defects of the Boer? some may be asking. While commenting on the different phases of the Boer character, we have alluded to and admitted many of these; for they are many. There is indeed much which we lament in the character of our people, and which we would, if it were possible, gladly alter or improve upon. Not all of them are good patriots, saints and heroes. Neither are all resourceful, kind-hearted, hospitable, and attached to their homes. There were "National Scouts," traitors, renegades, among the burghers! Among the women there were, alas! some, not many, who yielded to temptation. Such characters are found among all nations. Among the Boers they formed a small minority, and were the exceptions and not the general rule.

CHAPTER X

THE RISING IN THE CAPE COLONY

Having been in the full tide of the emotions of the Cape Colony—emotions which led to the taking up of arms—we feel ourselves justified in setting down those things which were to the Cape Colonist the justification of a warlike and anti-British policy.

It is strange, when one bears in mind that England admittedly extends greater liberties to her colonies than most other Powers, that many of her subjects are a continual source of trouble and fear to her. How has this to be accounted for? Is it because the colonists enjoy such great liberty (?) and share in so many privileges? Or is it because so many of them became British subjects *only because* they were compelled to take an oath of allegiance (or sign a declaration) to a government they neither loved nor respected but hated and despised? In the former case it would be base ingratitude on their part to rise in rebellion, in the latter it seems almost natural. However it be, the lustre and beauty of English history is sadly marred by the fact that often British artillery had to bear on British subjects, and British arms had to be employed to subdue England's own children.

Scotland, Ireland, Canada, the United States of America,

India, Afghanistan, Egypt, South Africa, and many besides of less importance, have resisted British authority at different times. Some of these, like the late Republics, were at one time or other laid in ruins and devastated by British arms. For years and years their inhabitants were subjected to awful persecutions. The blood of the best and bravest was spilt like water, whilst millions were spent to conquer whole populations—millions which might have been used for better and nobler purposes. And to-day thousands of British subjects are ruled by the point of the bayonet—by sheer force, not by common consent.

Having spent the greater part of the Anglo-Boer war time in the Cape Colony, we had the opportunity of ascertaining some, if not all, of the reasons why so many Colonial British subjects took up arms against the forces of their lawful king and sovereign. These causes we shall here narrate. By doing this we do not justify the action of those whose sympathies led them to cast in their lot with the two Republics. We do not wish to inculcate or foster the spirit of rebellion in any man, nor to fan it by words of approval. But we do wish to make known to the British public in particular that those Dutch colonists who sided with the late Republics during the lamentable war did not do so because they hated British rule or government or longed to shed the blood of English fellow-subjects. Neither did they enlist in our ranks because they regarded war as an adventurous game and mere child's play. In most cases the rebels were, prior to the war, as loyal to the British crown, and as devoted to British rule, as their fellow-English colonists ever were or could have been. For they had been born and brought up under the British flag; they knew no other, desired no better, even gloried in the flag of England. To it they looked for succour and protection in the hour of danger. Before the war the very men who fought against the British would have volunteered their services, at a moment's notice, to the Home Government if England was threatened in any way. Most of them, we are sure, would have willingly sacrificed their goods, and even lives, to shield the interests of the British Empire.

Now when these Dutch colonists took up arms they did not do so blindly, but fully realised the grave responsibility involved in such a step. They knew that the action was treasonable, and that, when captured, they were liable to the utmost penalty of the law, such as confiscation of goods, banishment, imprisonment for life, or death. Some of them, before they enlisted, had been compelled by the military authorities to be present at the execution of those who had unfortunately fallen into the hands of the enemy. In spite of that most tangible warning, they nevertheless joined the Boer ranks. What then were their reasons for risking their very lives in a cause which might perhaps fail? Surely such men as rose in rebellion had potent and valid reasons! To be stigmatised for life by the title of rebel could not be deemed so great an honour as to induce a man to face all the dangers and hardships of war. Nor were these colonial rebels mercenaries; they were volunteers, that came to the assistance of two small republics.

Those who were acquainted with the situation and with the political parties at the Cape prior to the war expected and dreaded, in the event of war with the Republics, a general outbreak in the Cape Colony, and were not surprised when their expectations proved true.

The Cape Dutch, as well as their English neighbours, knew only too well that, in the event of war, the whole of South Africa would suffer, that the flames of it would spread far beyond the Republican borders, and would be kindled in the adjoining British colonies. Thoroughly convinced that that would be the result of a war on the two Republics they did all in their power to prevent it. Had the English element in

South Africa been as eager as the Dutch to abide in peace and avoid bloodshed, there certainly never would have been war. But, alas! one party had set its heart upon it.

To precipitate matters and bring them to a crisis, the public in England was inflamed by rumours of the wildest nature, and was, unfortunately, enticed to believe anything and everything which was reported. British interests, British paramountcy, etc., were supposed to be seriously threatened by a great Pan-Africander conspiracy, which had for its objective the total elimination of the Imperial factor in South Africa. The Dutch were plotting, so it was rumoured, to oust the British from South Africa by driving them all into the sea on a certain day. What a preposterous absurdity! And many were so innocent as to believe and fear that a small nation of farmers would actually attempt to expel the British from South Africa. The Boer may be ignorant, but he has more common sense than to give such an idea even a thought.

The Cape Dutch, we are glad to state, left no stone unturned in their attempts to avert a war on a kindred race which was bound to prove calamitous to, and inflict endless misery on, thousands. Whilst diplomatic negotiations went on between the Transvaal and English Governments, and it became evident that these negotiations would in all probability result in failure, Mr. Jan Hofmeyer,—"onze Jan," that far-seeing, famous Cape politician,—and Mr. Harold, M.P., left for Pretoria, and by the co-operation of President Steyn prevailed on President Kruger to submit those proposals to the British Government which the Colonial Secretary frankly admitted might form the basis of a peaceful settlement. "We have nine-tenths of what we wanted," the Colonial Secretary is reported to have said, "and the other tenth is not worth our going to war for." Sad that that one-tenth should have demanded the lives of thousands of men, women and children, millions of pounds, besides ruin and misery to so many!

When war seemed inevitable and its declaration only a matter of time, the Africander Party, which then constituted the majority in the Cape Parliament, passed a resolution in Parliament, by which they solemnly protested against any aggressive policy on the part of the Imperial Government. They pointed out to the Home Government what endless woes a war would entail, and how detrimental it would prove to Imperial interests through the length and breadth of South Africa. At the same time they stated, in the most unequivocal language, their strong disapproval of extreme and coercive measures. This protest was slighted. The members who subscribed their names to it, and who represented the feeling of the Cape Dutch, were called disloyal. For to be loyal in those days meant to side with the war party, and approve of all they said and did. To think independently, and to express one's political views frankly and fearlessly, was a sure sign of disloyalty, when one's aims were for a peaceful solution of the difficulties of the moment.

Besides this Parliamentary resolution, the Cape Dutch drew up a large petition, addressed to Queen Victoria, whom they all loved as a mother and revered as a Queen. This petition was signed by thousands of women, who entreated their gracious and tender Mother-Queen to refrain from a policy which would result in bloodshed. This plea for peace and justice also failed to accomplish anything. The voice of the Dutch colonists was not heeded. Their petitions and protests were ignored and rejected time and again. The petition, however, of some 21,000 Uitlanders in Johannesburg, who clamoured for redress of grievances, immediately called forth armed intervention!

This, then, was the attitude of the Cape Dutch before the declaration of war: emphatic disapproval of any war policy. They disapproved of and protested against war in South Africa, not because they were disloyal, and had not the interests of the mother-country at heart, or because they naturally sympathised with the Boers as being a kindred race. They declared themselves against the Imperial war policy, because they knew and were confident that it was by no means impossible to arrive at a peaceful solution of all difficulties and disputes along friendly diplomatic lines, by which the actual grievances of British subjects in Johannesburg could be redressed, and political affairs so adjusted that it would not be necessary to shed one drop of blood. So far from being disloyal, they prided themselves in being British subjects, and, as such, they claimed the rights and privileges to which all British subjects are entitled. Their services in the interests of peace were, however, not appreciated, but were construed into acts calculated to encourage the enemy and to foster rebellion.

The Press had declared war months before it was actually proclaimed. Feeling ran so high that men would not listen to reason. "Fight it out," was the frantic cry of many, who had not the remotest idea of what "fighting it out" meant.

Though frustrated in their endeavours to prevent the threatened war, the Cape Dutch, after hostilities had once begun, tried very hard to bring about a speedy termination of the struggle, and to effect a settlement which would be honourable to English and Dutch alike, and which would secure all, if not more than all, that the English had ever demanded.

Let us note some of the steps they took.

When the Imperial Government announced their policy of annexation of the Republics after the occupation of Bloemfontein and Pretoria, the voice of the Cape Dutch was raised once more. They knew that Lord Roberts had greatly mistaken the character of the people he had come to conquer when he thought that no sooner would their capitals be occupied by his forces than all the Boers would surrender. They were conscious of the fact that a war of annexation would lead to one of conquest, and that the Boers, rather than sacrifice their independence, would choose to fight to the finish. Hence the colonial Dutch again strongly urged the Home Government to discard the policy of annexation, which would crush and destroy the national life of two small states, which had bravely fought and struggled for their independent existence.

A conference, attended by thousands representing the whole Dutch population of the Cape Colony, was held at Worcester on the 6th of December, 1900. In that conference or congress of the people resolutions were unanimously adopted discountenancing the policy which led to the annexation of the two Republics. Six prominent men were chosen from the Worcester delegates, and were deputed to go and appeal to the conscience of the English people. It was hoped that, at least, in England—the home of liberty—they would be allowed to plead their cause, and lay it bare before the public. How enthusiastically (?) they were received in England and Scotland is well known. *Warm* receptions were extended to them. "Away with them! Crucify them!" was the cry of the enraged war party. Instead of their message being listened to, these men were mobbed, hissed at and hooted; sometimes they had to flee so as not to be the targets for the missiles of the mob. And the treatment of these men, who represented at least 90,000 Dutch colonists, at the hands of their fellow-British subjects, was that not an insult—a mockery of liberty and equal rights?

Besides this deputation of the people, two of the leading ministers of the Cape Parliament—Messrs. Merriman and Sauer—went to England on a similar errand, but fared no better. In vain did they offer their services to the Imperial

Parliament by way of suggesting a basis for a settlement, which would terminate a war of devastation and ruination. The war party would have none of them. Forsooth, they too were traitors, working against British interests!

The women-folk at the Cape were as anxious as the men, first to prevent, and then to stop, the unfortunate war, the burdens of which they shared with their husbands. Three times large numbers of them met in conference, at Paarl, Worcester and Cape Town, and there they fearlessly and strongly protested against the conduct of the war and the annexation of the two Republics. Through the medium of these conferences they expostulated and pleaded with the Home Government to abstain from what they rightly regarded as a stupendous crime, the annihilation of two small states by overwhelming forces. Their petitions, if they ever reached the British Government, were treated with silent contempt. Did they merit such treatment?

All this and much more was done in the interests of peace by the Dutch colonists. Both before and during the war they did all they possibly could to rescue or redeem South Africa from the horrors and calamities of a disastrous war. They failed. Was it their fault? Was it right to brand as rebels and traitors every Cape Colonial that protested against the war, and refused to assist the mighty British Empire against the Republics?

The Africander Bond—a political organization at the Cape—was the scape-goat during the war. Those who were in search of a pretext for the cause of the war and its continuation found it in this organization. Everything that was low and mean was laid to the charge of the Africander Bond. Its unwearied efforts to induce the English to terminate a war, declared and carried on in direct opposition to the wishes of tens of thousands of England's devoted subjects, were construed into being so many encouragements for the Republicans to continue the struggle. The Worcester conference was said to have encouraged and invited General De Wet to invade the Colony—an invasion which was planned long *before* the conference was held, and which failed in the first instance, and only succeeded three months after the conference had met!

When all the efforts of the Cape Dutch failed, and the voice of the people was not regarded but systematically suppressed, it is not strange that there were men who found it impossible to remain silent and inactive in such circumstances. Gradually their loyalty was being undermined. The strain placed upon it was too great; it was stretched to the breaking point. They enlisted and took the field against the forces of that Government which they once loved so well, and then—despised.

This brings us to some of the more direct causes of the colonial rebellion, which we shall enumerate in succession. The war with the Republics was an aggression on a *kindred race*, and was declared and conducted to the extreme displeasure, and in direct opposition to the wishes, of the Dutch colonists, who spared themselves neither pain nor trouble to ward off or terminate a war which was bound to inflict great misery on themselves, and on thousands with whom they were intimately connected by ties of blood and friendship. For are the Transvaal and Free State Boers not the sons and daughters of those pioneers that emigrated from the Cape Colony between the years 1834-40, in search of an independent home beyond the Orange and Vaal rivers? Moreover, among the burghers of the Republics there were several colonists who, prior to the war, had settled in the Transvaal, chiefly in Johannesburg and Pretoria, as well as in the Orange Free State. These colonial settlers constituted another link in the chain which bound the Cape Dutch to the

Boers. They regarded the Republics as their native land, and consequently came to their assistance in the hour of danger. There they had found a home, acquired wealth in some instances, and thus would not desert them when their services were most needed. Instead of abandoning the two Republics to their sad fate, they were determined to support them with all the energy and power at their command. On the battlefield many of them distinguished themselves by their dauntless valour. They willingly sacrificed their lives and property for their adopted fatherland, which they loved even better than many a Boer. For when the Boers became disheartened and surrendered ignominiously, the Colonials, be it said to their everlasting honour, remained steadfast, thereby putting to shame those burghers who were possessed of so little national pride as to kneel at the invaders' feet and sue for mercy.

These Transvaal and Free State Colonials had their relatives in the Cape Colony, so that the Dutch of South Africa may almost be regarded as one large family, linked together from Table Bay to the Zambezi by bonds of blood, religion and marriage. Hence it was impossible to strike a blow at the two states without touching the very heart of the Cape Dutch—impossible to inflict losses and bring ruin upon some members of the family without seriously disturbing and distressing the rest. The physical boundaries separating the British colonies from the Republics made no separation as far as the people were concerned. In speech, religion, character, and blood, the Dutch are essentially one throughout South Africa. And it was owing to this fact that the Cape Dutch felt for the Republicans as none else could have felt. Their strong sympathies took the form of practical assistance when they shouldered their rifles and took the field against the enemies of the Republics. But this was not done before their protests, petitions, and all other constitutional measures had signally failed, and were utterly ignored by the British Government. Then only did they resort to aggressive measures.

However strongly some might condemn their action, still we believe that any other people, even the English themselves, and they probably to a far greater extent, would, in like circumstances, have acted similarly. If England had been invaded by a foreign foe, and English homes destroyed and burnt *en masse*, and English women and children removed in thousands to disease-stricken camps, and English officers and soldiers court-martialled or deported to distant islands and countries, we ask, would Scotland, for instance, have looked on with stolid indifference and cold apathy? Would she not, as well as all other true Englishmen, wherever they were, have protested most emphatically against such a war; and if their protests were slighted, would they not have assisted their fellow-Englishmen? Verily they would, were they subjects or not of the invaders.

This is exactly what the Cape Dutch did when some of them rose in rebellion. Their loyalty was gradually undermined as the war assumed the character of conquest and extermination. It was too much for many a Colonial to be a silent spectator when thousands of women and children pined away in concentration camps; and the military authorities, apparently wreaking vengeance on these because the burghers would not surrender, positively refused to allow these Boer families to reside with their relatives or friends in the Cape Colony, or live *at their own cost* in garrisoned towns, where they would have no intercourse with the burghers. When the weak and defenceless became the victims of the war, and received such treatment, the Cape Dutch were incited to violent actions. They rose to protect the weak against the strong, the few against the many. In so doing have they committed the unpardonable sin? Or will there be mercy even for these?

The Colonists were left unprotected at the tender mercy of the Boer forces. When the Boers, on the declaration of war, crossed the colonial borders and pushed ahead into British territory, they found the districts and most of the villages in an entirely defenceless condition. The garrison of Aliwal North consisted of three Cape policemen. Colesberg, Venterstad, Burghersdorp, Lady Grey, James Town, Dordrecht, Rhodes, and many other places were occupied one after the other, without being in the least protected. In Natal, Griqualand West, and British Bechuanaland it was not any better.

The Colonists thought that they were subjects of a vast and mighty empire, to which they could confidently look for protection against invaders. If they had any fears, these were hushed, for surely the mother-country was powerful enough to shelter them from the withering blasts of war. To their astonishment the mother-country could protect neither their persons nor their property, but entrusted all to the care of the Boer commandoes. Had the Colonists no claim to protection? Was it their fault that the British Government had accepted an ultimatum before they were prepared to extend to their colonial subjects that protection to which they certainly had a lawful claim? Such questions the Colonists asked themselves and the Home Government.

Left unprotected, and literally forsaken for months by their own Government, they yielded to the temptation to make common cause with the Boers, whom they met and saw daily. They enlisted in considerable numbers, and so cast in their lot for better or for worse with the Boers. Still the majority of the colonial farmers remained at home, and those who joined the Boer ranks at the commencement of the war were, as a rule, commandeered or called up. By proclamation all Colonists who resided within the occupied territory received the option either of leaving it within a certain time, or of staying, on condition of submitting to the Martial Law regulations of the new Government.

Under this strange thing, called Martial Law, these Colonists were summoned to join the ranks of the Boers. In how far this action of commandeering Colonists was commendable on the part of the Republics is difficult to say for one not versed in all the technicalities of International Law, or in the terms prescribed by the various Conventions. It seemed, however, that as far as the Republics were concerned, International Law and Convention obligations did not exist at all. The policy of the Republics all through the war, as one might expect, was to secure and maintain the friendship and sympathy of their colonial brethren. The Colonist was treated as a friend, and not as an enemy. His person and property were respected so long as he remained neutral. Strict neutrality, and nothing more, the Boers enjoined, especially towards the end of the war.

To be fair towards the Republics, we have to note that when the Colonists were commandeered at the commencement of the war—for it was *only then*, and not later, that they were summoned to the front—the object of the States was not to force them into their service. It was more a precautionary measure to protect the Colonist should he fall into the hands of the enemy. The fact that he had been commandeered, when taken into account, might, and did, tend to mitigate his punishment. This commandeering was never rigorously enforced. Occasionally officers acting on their own responsibility, and without instructions from the Boer governments, commandeered and pressed Colonists to take up arms without their consent; but such cases were exceptional, and were disapproved of. What the Boers wanted were men who volunteered their services, and came to them, not because they were disloyal to their Government, but because such a strain was laid upon them that they were compelled to come. Upon such men they could rely, and they proved themselves worthy of the confidence placed in them.

The various war proclamations issued by the British from time to time goaded the Colonists into rebellion.

If all the proclamations which were circulated in the Republics and British colonies were published they would constitute a volume of no mean dimensions, and might afford instructive reading "to principalities and powers" planning to enlarge their dominions by the assistance, and on the basis, of proclamations. In South Africa these "paper sheets" were by far the most formidable allies of the British Empire. They wrought greater havoc among the Boer forces than all the British batteries ever did; for when they first began to explode in the midst of the burghers the latter dropped down thick and fast. Thousands were lured away from the posts of duty by the fascinating and seemingly generous proposals contained in some proclamations. Had the Field-Marshal only understood the Boer character better, and strictly adhered to his first proclamation, and not violated its conditions, and replaced it by others calculated to harass the surrendered Boer to such an extent that war, with all its hardships and dangers, seemed preferable to a life of continual dread and vexation, thousands of surrendered burghers who enlisted would assuredly never have fired a shot at the British troops. And it is just possible that that proclamation would have secured victory for the British arms at a much earlier date had it been abided by with more discretion. But then others came in quick succession. And so it often happened that by proclamation a burgher would be disarmed while another would compel ten others to take the field. They were undoubtedly the best commandeering agents the Boers ever had. Thousands of Boers and Colonists were from time to time commandeered by the stringent and drastic obligations imposed upon them by these proclamations. On the other hand they facilitated matters very greatly for the enemy. Where the soldier could not go the proclamation was sent; what the former could not do the latter often successfully accomplished. Officers and burghers who had baffled the enemy by their movements, and had routed them time and again, were captured by—proclamations.

Everything and anything the enemy required was secured by proclamation. Horses, mules, donkeys, oxen, ammunition, rifles, barley, wheat, hay, corn, maize, vehicles, and even luxuries, such as sugar, jams, etc., were all gathered in by—proclamations. Besides, by proclamation the non-combatant farmer, who was supposed to be neutral, was compelled to report, at the nearest column or British post, the presence or whereabouts of any armed Boer or Boers that he might happen to know of—and that immediately, even at the risk of being shot should he fall into the hands of the enemy he was reporting. Losing his life was, of course, a matter of little consequence to the British.

When the enemy adopted such tactics, the Boers had to counteract their proclamations by circulating others. Now in doing that the non-combatants were placed between two fires. They had to serve two masters in carrying out the instructions of proclamations diametrically opposed to each other. The man who was ingenious enough to act a double part, who could steer clear of Charybdis and Scylla, alone evaded trouble. There were, however, not many who succeeded in pleasing or duping both parties for any length of time.

The Boer proclamations levelled at those of the English made it specially irksome to the Colonists, who were finally encompassed by a host of proclamations. When they failed to obey the English proclamations they were fined, cast into gaol, and treated as criminals. When they obeyed the

English, and consequently violated the Boer proclamations, they had to undergo the penalty, fines, corporal punishment, and even death, imposed by the Boers. The English said: "This do, and thou shalt live"; the Boers: "This do not, and thou shalt live."

As far as possible the Colonists were left unmolested on their farms by the Boers, who expected them, as non-combatants, to remain strictly neutral. The English proclamations, on the other hand, converted these non-combatant farmers into scouts, and often into spies. They had to give the enemy every information concerning the Boer commandoes—as to their strength, the condition of their horses, the number of unarmed burghers, of servants, their movements and plans, as far as they could discover these, etc., etc. In some instances they were commandeered to take upon themselves the dangerous responsibility of acting as guides to the British columns, and were then dismissed to return to their farms and pose as non-combatants. This the Boers could not tolerate, and had to prevent by forbidding it through counter-proclamations, which the enemy laughed to scorn. The unfortunate farmer could not similarly slight and ignore them. He *had* to obey them, or abide the consequences.

When the Colonists were subjected to vexations of such a serious nature, and when the British persisted in rigorously enforcing their proclamations, the position of the Colonists became untenable and drove them into rebellion. Had the military authorities exercised greater wisdom and more common sense, so many British subjects would not have fallen away. There were colonial rebels who never, never would have lifted a rifle, whose loyalty was beyond all questioning, but the pressure laid upon them by proclamations so numerous, onerous and odious in character, forced them to fight for or against the Boers. To do the former would be disloyal and treasonable, to acquiesce in the latter would be violating the dictates of conscience. Was it the fault of the Colonists that they were placed in such an awkward position?

Martial Law and the way it was administered has been one of the leading causes of the colonial rebellion. As long as the Colonists were permitted to express their sentiments or political views through the medium of congresses, conferences, public meetings, resolutions and petitions, they cherished the hope that the Home Government would eventually listen to their pleas. But when Martial Law was declared, the constitution of the Cape Colony was virtually suspended, and the Colonists were deprived of most, if not all, of their liberties—liberties of speech, of the Press and of conscience. Under Martial Law none, not even the most loyal, were allowed to write or say anything which did not harmonize exactly with the views and actions of the Imperial Government as represented in South Africa. Now, when men may neither speak nor write, they are apt to act. The Colonists, being compelled by this most wonderful of all laws—if law it be at all—acted. For this law justified all things, as far as the war party was concerned, while it condemned the rest indiscriminately. It gave armed men unlimited power over the unarmed. It allowed the strong to crush the weak, the rich to rob the poor, and the scoundrel to lodge in gaol the man of honour and reputation. Nothing so exasperated the Colonists as the odious manner in which the Martial Law regulations were carried out, and nothing made greater rebels than the harshness of these regulations.

As the situation in the Cape Colony became more and more serious, the most arbitrary and despotic methods were adopted to quell the rebellion by trying to intimidate the Colonists. The policy of the gallows was unscrupulously brought into practice, and the barbarous method of compelling the Dutch residents to attend the execution of their fellow-Dutch was enforced. At Burghersdorp, Cradock, Middelburg, and various other places several rebels were executed. The chief Dutch residents were compelled not only to listen to the public promulgation of these death sentences, but had also to be present at the execution. On July 10, 1901, the execution of one Marais took place at Middelburg. At 9 A.M. he was executed in the presence of the leading residents. Among these was Mr. De Waal, M.L.A., who entered the precincts of the gaol attired in deep mourning. The scene proved too much for him; he broke down completely before the executioner had drawn the bolt.

Now these tragic enactments influenced the Colonists in one of two ways. Some of them—the more timid—who were eye-witnesses of the executions of their fellow-Dutch, became so intimidated that nothing could induce them to take up arms against the British. Others—and these not a few—instead of being over-awed and frightened, got infuriated. In the awful presence of the gallows, on which their beloved countrymen ended their earthly career, there and then, as they gazed on them in silent sorrow, they took a solemn oath that, come what may, *avenge* they would the blood of their kindred. From the gallows they went to their different homes with impressions and feelings so deep and bitter that not even "Time's effacing finger" will be able to wipe them out for centuries to come. From these heart-rending scenes they turned their faces, and anxiously awaited the first Boer commando.

On one occasion no less than fifteen colonists, who were forced to attend the execution of a fellow-colonist, came to my commando and begged me to provide them with horses and rifles. Nothing could induce them to return, for they had seen a comrade slain, and that was sufficient. And so time and again colonists joined the Boer ranks because they had to witness scenes calculated to stir up the most callous and indifferent. If these were moved, how much more the hearts and hands of those linked by ties of blood and love to the fallen! One brother would enlist because the other was heavily fined or imprisoned simply on suspicion. Two or more colonists would club together and join the Boer ranks after a friend or relative of them had been executed. To cite a few instances:—

In the Middelburg district a certain farmer, by name Van Heerden, was commandeered by an English patrol to act as guide. Reluctantly he obeyed, and led the patrol to the best of his ability. Not far from his home the Boers opened fire on them. The British retreated, leaving their wounded behind. Van Heerden himself was dangerously wounded. He was carried off the field by his wife and servants and laid up in his house. A few days after the column to which the patrol belonged arrived at Van Heerden's farm. The officer in command entered the house of the wounded man in a raging temper, and ordered him to be carried out and shot immediately. In vain did the wife of Van Heerden expostulate and plead with the unmerciful officer to spare the life of her wounded husband. Van Heerden was carried out, tied to a chair placed beside a stone wall, and seven Lee-Metford bullets penetrated the brain of the man who was wounded, perhaps mortally, *in the service of the British army*! That was his reward. Even that did not satisfy those who thirsted for blood, for the house of the unfortunate man was forthwith looted, and his widow and orphans robbed of everything. A few days after this sad event had occurred our commando arrived at the same farm. The spot where the victim sat was pointed out to me; the marks of the bullets, the blood and the brain against the wall were still distinctly discernible, and seemed to cry to heaven for revenge. And there was the family of the departed—stripped of everything. The burghers contributed from their scanty means what they could in support of the widow and orphans.

No wonder that the brothers of this unfortunate man took up arms and became the most pronounced, the most bitter enemies of those who ruthlessly slew, if not murdered, their brother. One of them—Jacobus van Heerden—whenever he spoke of his brother's death, would bite his lips, his face would flush, and one could hear him mutter: "My brother's blood shall be avenged." In the whole commando there was not a more dauntless man than he. But, alas! he too passed away. A bullet was destined to pierce his skull. At a farm, Leeuwfontein, in the district of Murraysburg, he was shot by a Kaffir.

On another occasion four Colonists were arrested; two of these were shot in cold blood, while the other two were imprisoned, *because* the railway line was blown up and a train derailed by the Boers near their home. They were accused of having known all about the Boers, who had destroyed the railway line *during the night*—an accusation which, on later investigation, proved false.

When such crimes were perpetrated in the name of Martial Law, we are rather surprised that all the Colonists did not rise to a man. What would the English have done if subjected to such treatment? The Dutchman is naturally slow to move, and very patient. He seems born to suffer and endure. But Martial Law imposed such heavy burdens upon him that he could not but resent them. Where the Boers were too lax in enforcing their Martial Law regulations, the English went to the other extreme in applying theirs too strenuously.

Well may we ask whether it was a wise policy which converted so many Colonists into bitter enemies, by subjecting them to such revolting measures.

The enlisting of blacks by the British induced many Colonists to cast in their lot with the Boers. If natives were to be employed to crush a kindred race, the Colonists thought that they were justified in rendering assistance to their fellow-Dutch.

Moreover, these armed natives, once promoted to the rank of soldiers, tantalized the farmers, who were formerly their masters, to an inconceivable degree. With rifle in hand they would go to these and treat them in the most insulting manner. They would commandeer bread, butter, milk, clothes, horses, and everything else they pleased, and woe to the man or woman that did not promptly answer their demands.

The farmers of the Western Province of the Cape Colony suffered perhaps most in this respect. The natives had all congregated in the villages, and there they were armed to assist in the work of destruction, while the farmer, who required their services, had to tend his flocks and plough his fields all alone.

In Calvinia was an infamous Hottentot column, five hundred strong. These Hottentots were the scare and plague of the whole district. By their actions they goaded the Calvinia farmers into rebellion.

Let us summarize these causes mentioned—causes which to some extent account for the rising in the Cape Colony. They were:—

(*a*) War on a kindred race without consent of Colonists.

(*b*) The Colonists left unprotected, and thus exposed to danger and temptation.

(*c*) The Colonists harassed by multitudinous proclamations and (*d*) Subjected to embarrassing Martial Law regulations.

(*e*) The arming of natives against Colonists and Republicans.

Other causes why so many once loyal and devoted British subjects took up arms against the English may be cited, but the aforementioned are the principal ones. By enumerating them we express neither approval nor disapproval of the action of the Colonists; for we admire nothing more in friend or foe than unfeigned devotion and loyalty to country and people. The traitor and renegade are to be pitied, and their actions despised. We could not but admire the loyalty of many a colonist under such untoward circumstances; when that loyalty was stretched to the breaking-point, when it became impossible for them to remain such any longer, then and then only we gladly welcomed them and equipped them as best we could.

Those who stigmatize the Colonists as traitors, rebels, or renegades, would do well to take into account the peculiar position in which they were placed by the war, before passing a rash judgment on them. To be fair towards the Colonists we must take into consideration the causes which produced the effects. Only after a thorough investigation of the causes could a just sentence be passed on the colonial rebel. If governments have no responsibility whatever towards their subjects or citizens, and no binding obligations to fulfil in respect to them, then only may the investigation of causes be discarded.

None lament more the sad results of the South African war than the writers of these pages. Before the war Dutch and English lived and worked side by side as friends and brothers. The two races, once hostile, began to understand and respect one another more and more. In the schools the Dutch and English languages had equal rights. In some

Dutch Reformed Churches English sermons were delivered by Dutch pastors to Dutch and English congregations. The railways of the Free State were almost exclusively controlled by English officials. In the Government offices Dutch and English clerks worked together. The principal villages of the Orange Free State were almost more English than Dutch. The British subjects were perfectly content with the Free State Government and desired no better. In the Transvaal the state of affairs was much the same. Before the Jameson Raid there existed a kindly feeling between Dutch and English. If time and patience had only been exercised, no blood would have been shed, there never would have been war in South Africa. But what time and patience would have wrought, the war party undertook when they plunged the land into a war the effects of which will be felt by more than one generation.

Thousands of British subjects have been estranged from the mother-country and turned into implacable enemies by the war. In many a home there is a vacant chair, and round many a fireside one is missing at eventide. Several families, once so happy and content, now mourn the irreparable loss of a father or brother, a mother or sister. Thousands, who were well-to-do before the war, are now poverty-stricken. Who then shall adequately depict the misery and woe which has entered so many homes since the first shot was fired in South Africa? And to-day, when the roar of cannons, the din of rifles and the clatter of arms have been hushed, there are men pining away in foreign countries because they may not return to their native land. There are the unhappy exiles in Belgium, Holland, France and America. Their families are left to the mercy and care of friends and relatives in South Africa. How their hearts are yearning to go to these, but...! Besides these exiles there are those undergoing sentences of penal servitude either for life or for long periods. There are the burghers in Bermuda and in India who, because they cannot conscientiously take an oath of allegiance to the British

Government, are not allowed to return to their native land. As I ponder over the condition of these unhappy cases my heart seems to break, and a feeling of compassion mingled with sorrow inexpressible rises in my bosom.

While referring to these, I would dare to plead earnestly with the Imperial Government to display mercy and generosity. Exercise these towards the exiled, not only for their sake, but also for the sake of their families and for the promotion of peace in South Africa. Is it too much to plead for a general amnesty? Will that not lessen the intense race-hatred between two peoples destined to live in the same land?

True reconciliation is the foundation on which the structure of a united South Africa shall be raised. Without reconciliation there can be no co-operation, and South Africa will be in the future what it has been in the past—a land of strife and discord. Adhere to a policy of severity and the gulf between Dutch and English will grow deeper and deeper as the years roll by. There will be another Ireland, instead of a land where "peace and rest for ever dwell."

CHAPTER XI

WAR INCIDENTS

Notwithstanding the horror and depression which must necessarily keep step with the campaigner, death staring him in the face throughout the campaign, yet the burgher endeavoured to show a cheerful countenance. In this he succeeded to a surprising degree. It is a characteristic of the Boer that he can meet frowning fortune with a smile or at least a shrug of the shoulders. He found that his best policy was to forget the reverse of yesterday. Flying to-day before the enemy, to-morrow he will rally, and charge that same foe with almost irresistible determination.

In this, the last chapter, we want to dwell not on the tragic aspects of the war, but on its lighter side. Gradually we learnt to be more conscious of the amusing than of the sad scenes of the battlefield. Months of fighting, if they had hardened our natures, had yet left us the power of laughter.

The South African War was rich in incidents that tended to lighten our burdens. Hardly a day passed by without something happening, either on the battlefield or in the camp, which caused us amusement. The burghers, in spite of looks and behaviour, had a keen sense of humour. Even when we were so hotly pressed that there was often no pause made for a meal, a joke in the saddle was relished in the place of food. In little groups, too, round the camp fires we would beguile the long evenings of winter nights by relating our personal adventures. We will record a few of these, acquired from personal experience or overheard at such gatherings.

Moving in the Reddersburg district, we camped for a night at a dam which contained a small quantity of water. The next morning the burghers, discovering that there were fish in the pool, but having no fishing-hooks, undressed and began to convert the water into a muddy mass, thus compelling the fish to come to the surface for air. While still engaged in this impromptu fishing, with bodies mud-covered from top to toe, they heard the cry "Opzaal! opzaal! Khakis near by." So near was the enemy that they could not afford to lose a minute. As there was neither clean water nor time to wash off the mud, they were obliged to jump into their clothes, besmeared as they were with mud. It was an amusing sight to see them running to their clothes, black as negroes, and, regardless of the mud, dressing as quickly as they could. Some of them had a very narrow escape, and not before sunset could they take another bath.

The destruction of the railway-line afforded us much fun. There were burghers who dreaded this kind of work much more than actual fighting. They would rather get into the firing-line than go to the railway-line. They feared nothing so much as to handle a charge of dynamite, by which the destruction was usually accomplished. To prevent any accidents, a whistle was blown as a signal to apply the lights to all the fuses at once, so that the men could all withdraw to a safe distance before the explosion took place. On one occasion a burgher, intentionally or out of fright, lit his fuse while the others were still engaged depositing their charges under the rails. The surprise of the rest on seeing the fuse alight took the form of helter-skeltering away, some rushing against the railway fence, others almost breaking their necks over ant-heaps, while some only got away a few yards before the explosion took place. Fortunately none were injured, and when all was over they laughed heartily over their own disorderly retreat.

After we had blown up the line we went to a farm about three miles away. As we halted in front of the door, the farmer's wife—her husband had been deported—came out. The old lady appeared very agitated; she begged us kindly to leave as soon as possible. It seemed she was entertaining three English soldiers as guests that night, and was anxious that we should not disturb their slumbers, which action would get her into trouble. "Oh, do go," she said, "for if you disturb these sleeping guests, I also will be prosecuted and sent to India." Poor soul! She was doing her best to protect her visitors, not because she cared so much for them, but for fear of the consequences should we lay hands on them. We could not, however, listen to her plea. We did not want Tommy himself, but only his rifle and ammunition. Hence we went to their room and found them sharing one bed. It was midnight and so they did not expect us at all. Imagine their feelings on realizing that armed Boers surrounded their bed! Their complete helplessness, as they lay undressed and unarmed, caused the burghers to indulge in hearty laughter. To silence their fears we assured them that they need not dread any evil, we would soon dismiss them.

Our military councils were frequently occasions of humour—a grim humour which could only appeal to the Boer, made grim by the treachery of fellow-Dutchmen.

At the beginning of the war some, especially the uninitiated, dreaded nothing more than a war council. To such it was a body of men invested with unlimited power, a council that could pronounce sentence of death on whomsoever they wished. To appear before this august assembly meant almost certain death. Now sometimes it meant that, but more often not. For one reason or another prisoners were for the time being brought in under a wrong impression of the character of the assembly. Such was the case with two farmers in the district of Trompsburg, Orange River Colony. They had been arrested on a charge of sending reports to the enemy. Terror-stricken, they appeared before the war council, there to render an account of their deeds. Before their trial began, the president of the council, in addressing the other officers, assured them that whatever sentence they should consider just would be carried out by him. If sentence of death should be passed, he would not hesitate to take his rifle and put an end to the lives of the accused. "We must," he said, "put a stop to these treasonable acts." The poor prisoners trembled from head to foot. No mercy! On being examined, they acknowledged that they had forwarded treasonable reports to the enemy, and began to plead for mercy. One of them asked us to bear in mind that he was a poor man, and had a wife and a large family that would be left destitute. Pretending to be quite in earnest, we assured him that we were decided to take nothing into consideration, and would mete out strict justice. They were then removed so that the court could decide on their punishment. After a few minutes' consultation they were called in, and asked to subscribe their names to a statement which ran as follows:—

> We, the undersigned, do hereby declare, that, as burghers of the Orange Free State, we had no right to send reports to the British, and, in doing so, we have committed High Treason.

When they had signed the paper one of the officers remarked that we must have such a declaration signed by the accused to justify our actions with regard to them before the

Government. Another officer asked the president whether the prisoners would be allowed to take leave of their families. To which the president abruptly replied: "No; such characters do not deserve any privileges." They were left under the awful impression for two hours that both would be shot, and then released with a warning to forward no reports to the enemy. Their anxiety must have been intense; their joy on being acquitted no less.

Non-combatants frequently found themselves in an uneasy and perplexing position. It was sometimes most difficult to differentiate between Boer and Briton, especially in the night. The poor farmer was often at his wits' end to know whom he was addressing, the more so when the British ranks were swelled by Dutch colonists and national scouts. The non-combatant farmer found it extremely difficult to steer a course inoffensive to either side. He was between two fires, for when suspected of disloyalty, either a Dutch or English trap might be laid for him. Not a few were caught in such snares. Others were more careful. If they did not know you personally, it was of no avail to tell them that you belonged to such and such a commando or column. They simply professed to know nothing. "I don't know," was the answer to every question. They were, of course, on the safe side. But many committed themselves, if not in deeds, then in words. To cite a few cases:—

One of our officers, Captain Pretorius, dismounted one evening at the farm of a Mr. B. in the district of Bethulie. The farmer, hearing a tap at the door, went and opened it. Pretorius, who posed as an English officer, asked Mr. B., "Where are the Boers?" The latter, pointing to certain ridges in the distance, said in rather broken English, "Do you see those kopjes yonder? They are full of Boers." But asked at the same time, "Do tell me, are you really an Englishman? I must be clear on this point before I can speak to you. There must be no mistake." On being assured by Pretorius and his party that they were not Boers and did not belong to the Boer forces, he told them very confidently all, and perhaps more than they wanted to know, for he began to express himself very strongly against the so-called marauding bands of Boers still roaming at large. He promised the supposed English officer that, as soon as possible, he would report the Boers; he would, he said, have done so already had the opportunity come his way. Just think how confused and embarrassed Mr. B. was when the English officer suddenly changed into a Boer, lifted his gun and said in his most harsh tone, "I feel inclined to send a bullet through your brains. Are you not ashamed to slander your own people in this way? It is because we have such Africanders as you in our midst that we suffer so much." This revelation proved almost too much for the farmer, who was of a timid and nervous disposition. The Boers left his farm the following day for regions so distant that it was impossible to trap him again. Once was enough for him.

The next victim resided in the same district. Commandant Joubert, having crossed the Bethulie-Springfontein line, touched at the farm of a certain Mr. X. Joubert, accompanied by a burgher, went to wake up Mr. X. They knocked loudly at the door; knocks failing, they were followed by a kick. But there was no response. Inside it was as still as the grave. Thinking that Mr. X. was out, the Commandant went to his brother's room, where he learnt that Mr. X. was in, sure enough. When Joubert heard this he went back to his room, tapped loudly once more, and then said, "Bring the dynamite, and let us blow up the show," while the other burgher said, "Never mind the dynamite, let us fire through the door." On hearing of dynamite and firing through the door, the occupant could remain silent no longer. He jumped up and cried out, "Wait, wait—don't fire! I am coming." Peeping out at the door, he asked with tremulous voice, "What do you want?" "Come out," said the Commandant; "I want to see you on important business." "The sooner you come the better for you," added the burgher, who happened to be related to Mr. X. This remark, however, spoiled the rest of the game, for Mr. X. recognised the voice of his relative, and catching at the same time a glimpse of his face in the bright moonlight, he rushed out and flung his arms around one who had not killed his relative's affection by his joke.

The following incident well illustrates the self-possession and presence of mind sometimes displayed by our opponents. On a certain day two Boer scouts were charged by two of their own men. The scouts, observing that the two burghers mistook them for enemies, simply dismounted and waited for them. While the two Boers came tearing up to their own scouts, two of the enemy's scouts who were not far off, observing these two Boers, took them in their turn for British, and thinking to render them some assistance, likewise charged the Boer scouts. When they reached the Boer scouts the two burghers had already captured (?) the latter, and had dismounted. Our friends at once realized their awkward position. They were in the presence of four Boers. Escape was out of the question, unless they could get round these Boers in some way or other. As both of them could talk Dutch, being Colonials, the happy idea struck them at once to try to pose as burghers, for there were several commandoes in that district, and it was just possible that these Boers, in whose hands they now were, would take their word and let them off. One of them, therefore, on reaching the burghers, very ingeniously remarked, "Well, you know, we actually took you for *khakis*." The other one was not slow to offer the burghers some fruit which he had in his pocket. And so they began talking to one another in a most familiar way. One of the Boers, a certain Mr. Bresler, suspected these two unknown friends, and while the other three were conversing with them as they sat on their horses, he (Bresler) kept his eyes on them, and watched their every movement. At length Bresler said, "Well, you had better go to your commando, or dismount your tired horses." Only too glad to get away they replied, "We are going; good-bye," and off they rode. "Do you know these fellows?" Bresler asked his comrades, as they were leaving them. "No," was the reply. "Well," said Bresler, "to be sure, they are British scouts." He called them back and asked them to which commando they belonged. "Potgieter's" was the answer. As there was no such commandant, they were immediately arrested. Had Bresler not been present the probability is that they would have captured the three burghers, for, as they told him, they simply waited for an opportunity to disarm them, but they saw that Bresler was watching them all the time and so could not venture to lift their rifles.

Sport of the most dangerous nature was sometimes indulged in. Certain Boer officers, and also privates, would risk their lives to have some amusement. Commandant W. Fouche was one of those who ventured most. Naturally brave and sometimes even reckless, he would step in almost anywhere. In the district of Willowmore, Cape Colony, he one evening entered a house where two of the enemy's scouts were comfortably seated by the side of two young ladies. He stepped into the room, greeted all, and took a seat next to one of the young ladies. To chafe and annoy the scouts, he placed his hand on the shoulder of one of the young ladies and pretended to kiss her. This act of his was enough to set one of the Englishmen on fire. "I shall not allow you," he said, "to touch the lady. You have no right to do it." Fouche then desisted; he withdrew his arm, and asked the young lady for some food, as he was very hungry. His friend calmed down, and they began to converse. By chance one of the scouts touched his pocket and noticed that there was something strange in it. "What is that hard thing in your pocket?" he queried. Fouche replied, "Oh, it is my pipe." "Your pipe is very large indeed," rejoined the scout. (This pipe was nothing else than a revolver.)

To irritate his unknown friends, Fouche began again to trifle with one of the ladies. This time the scout lost self-control; he rose, and taking his chair with both hands, brought it down upon Fouche with all his might, evidently with the intention of shattering the brains of the latter. Fouche smartly parried the blow, and the next instant the striker was a wounded man, and his comrade a prisoner.

In the district of Rouxville the same officer had a similar experience. There, one evening, he came across three of the enemy—one a Dutch colonist, the other two Britons—off-saddled at a farm. As they did not expect any Boers, their rifles were carelessly left outside the house. Fouche was again the one to enter. Having disguised himself so as to create no suspicion, he boldly walked in and shook hands with the party. The Colonial, in a domineering tone, asked him the object of his visit. "Come to see my young lady," was the reply. "Have you permission to leave your farm?" "No," said Fouche. "We arrest you at once," said the Colonial, "and will take you to Rouxville gaol. You shall have to walk all the way [some 24 miles], and that will teach you not to go about without a pass at this time of the night." "Well," said Fouche, "I really did not know that I must have a pass to come and see my young lady, and if you arrest me you must kindly allow me to get a horse at home, for certainly I cannot walk all this distance." "Nonsense," replied the Colonial; "there is no time to go home now."

As Fouche was supplicating for grace the other two went to fetch their horses. They were cordially received by the burghers outside. The Colonial in the meantime questioned Fouche as to the whereabouts of the Boers. The prisoner informed him that the notorious Commandant Fouche was again in that district. "Why," asked Fouche, "don't you capture this fellow with his raiding bands? They are the plague of the district. You should protect us." The Colonial: "Just a few days longer and he will be no more in the land of the living." At the same time he began to abuse him, without being conscious in the least that he was at the very moment speaking to that officer himself.

After some more talk he took Fouche by the arm and said, "Come along, we must be off; you are my prisoner." "What," rejoined the latter—"your prisoner! Don't you believe it. You are mine." So saying he took a revolver out of his pocket and pointed it at the over-confident Colonial, who thereupon looked several inches smaller.

Friedrich Kerst
Friedrich Nietzsche
Fyodor Dostoyevsky
G.A. Henty
G.K. Chesterton
Gabrielle E. Jackson
Garrett P. Serviss
Gaston Leroux
George A. Warren
George Ade
Geroge Bernard Shaw
George Cary Eggleston
George Durston
George Ebers
George Eliot
George Gissing
George MacDonald
George Meredith
George Orwell
George Sylvester Viereck
George Tucker
George W. Cable
George Wharton James
Gertrude Atherton
Gordon Casserly
Grace E. King
Grace Gallatin
Grace Greenwood
Grant Allen
Guillermo A. Sherwell
Gulielma Zollinger
Gustav Flaubert
H. A. Cody
H. B. Irving
H.C. Bailey
H. G. Wells
H. H. Munro
H. Irving Hancock
H. R. Naylor
H. Rider Haggard
H. W. C. Davis
Haldeman Julius
Hall Caine
Hamilton Wright Mabie
Hans Christian Andersen
Harold Avery
Harold McGrath
Harriet Beecher Stowe
Harry Castlemon
Harry Coghill
Harry Houidini
Hayden Carruth
Helent Hunt Jackson
Helen Nicolay
Hendrik Conscience
Hendy David Thoreau
Henri Barbusse
Henrik Ibsen
Henry Adams
Henry Ford
Henry Frost
Henry James
Henry Jones Ford
Henry Seton Merriman
Henry W Longfellow
Herbert A. Giles
Herbert Carter
Herbert N. Casson
Herman Hesse
Hildegard G. Frey
Homer
Honore De Balzac
Horace B. Day
Horace Walpole
Horatio Alger Jr.
Howard Pyle
Howard R. Garis
Hugh Lofting
Hugh Walpole
Humphry Ward
Ian Maclaren
Inez Haynes Gillmore
Irving Bacheller
Isabel Cecilia Williams
Isabel Hornibrook
Israel Abrahams
Ivan Turgenev
J.G.Austin
J. Henri Fabre
J. M. Barrie
J. M. Walsh
J. Macdonald Oxley
J. R. Miller
J. S. Fletcher
J. S. Knowles
J. Storer Clouston
J. W. Duffield
Jack London
Jacob Abbott
James Allen
James Andrews
James Baldwin
James Branch Cabell
James DeMille
James Joyce
James Lane Allen
James Lane Allen
James Oliver Curwood
James Oppenheim
James Otis
James R. Driscoll
Jane Abbott
Jane Austen
Jane L. Stewart
Janet Aldridge
Jens Peter Jacobsen
Jerome K. Jerome
Jessie Graham Flower
John Buchan
John Burroughs
John Cournos
John F. Kennedy
John Gay
John Glasworthy
John Habberton
John Joy Bell
John Kendrick Bangs
John Milton
John Philip Sousa
John Taintor Foote
Jonas Lauritz Idemil Lie
Jonathan Swift
Joseph A. Altsheler
Joseph Carey
Joseph Conrad
Joseph E. Badger Jr
Joseph Hergesheimer
Joseph Jacobs
Jules Vernes
Julian Hawthrone
Julie A Lippmann
Justin Huntly McCarthy
Kakuzo Okakura
Karle Wilson Baker
Kate Chopin
Kenneth Grahame
Kenneth McGaffey
Kate Langley Bosher
Kate Langley Bosher
Katherine Cecil Thurston
Katherine Stokes
L. A. Abbot
L. T. Meade

L. Frank Baum
Latta Griswold
Laura Dent Crane
Laura Lee Hope
Laurence Housman
Lawrence Beasley
Leo Tolstoy
Leonid Andreyev
Lewis Carroll
Lewis Sperry Chafer
Lilian Bell
Lloyd Osbourne
Louis Hughes
Louis Joseph Vance
Louis Tracy
Louisa May Alcott
Lucy Fitch Perkins
Lucy Maud Montgomery
Luther Benson
Lydia Miller Middleton
Lyndon Orr
M. Corvus
M. H. Adams
Margaret E. Sangster
Margret Howth
Margaret Vandercook
Margaret W. Hungerford
Margret Penrose
Maria Edgeworth
Maria Thompson Daviess
Mariano Azuela
Marion Polk Angellotti
Mark Overton
Mark Twain
Mary Austin
Mary Catherine Crowley
Mary Cole
Mary Hastings Bradley
Mary Roberts Rinehart
Mary Rowlandson
M. Wollstonecraft Shelley
Maud Lindsay
Max Beerbohm
Myra Kelly
Nathaniel Hawthrone
Nicolo Machiavelli
O. F. Walton
Oscar Wilde

Owen Johnson
P.G. Wodehouse
Paul and Mabel Thorne
Paul G. Tomlinson
Paul Severing
Percy Brebner
Percy Keese Fitzhugh
Peter B. Kyne
Plato
Quincy Allen
R. Derby Holmes
R. L. Stevenson
R. S. Ball
Rabindranath Tagore
Rahul Alvares
Ralph Bonehill
Ralph Henry Barbour
Ralph Victor
Ralph Waldo Emmerson
Rene Descartes
Ray Cummings
Rex Beach
Rex E. Beach
Richard Harding Davis
Richard Jefferies
Richard Le Gallienne
Robert Barr
Robert Frost
Robert Gordon Anderson
Robert L. Drake
Robert Lansing
Robert Lynd
Robert Michael Ballantyne
Robert W. Chambers
Rosa Nouchette Carey
Rudyard Kipling
Saint Augustine
Samuel B. Allison
Samuel Hopkins Adams
Sarah Bernhardt
Sarah C. Hallowell
Selma Lagerlof
Sherwood Anderson
Sigmund Freud
Standish O'Grady
Stanley Weyman
Stella Benson
Stella M. Francis

Stephen Crane
Stewart Edward White
Stijn Streuvels
Swami Abhedananda
Swami Parmananda
T. S. Ackland
T. S. Arthur
The Princess Der Ling
Thomas A. Janvier
Thomas A Kempis
Thomas Anderton
Thomas Bailey Aldrich
Thomas Bulfinch
Thomas De Quincey
Thomas Dixon
Thomas H. Huxley
Thomas Hardy
Thomas More
Thornton W. Burgess
U. S. Grant
Upton Sinclair
Valentine Williams
Various Authors
Vaughan Kester
Victor Appleton
Victor G. Durham
Victoria Cross
Virginia Woolf
Wadsworth Camp
Walter Camp
Walter Scott
Washington Irving
Wilbur Lawton
Wilkie Collins
Willa Cather
Willard F. Baker
William Dean Howells
William le Queux
W. Makepeace Thackeray
William W. Walter
William Shakespeare
Winston Churchill
Yei Theodora Ozaki
Yogi Ramacharaka
Young E. Allison
Zane Grey

www.ingramcontent.com/pod-product-compliance
Lightning Source LLC
Chambersburg PA
CBHW020551310726
48979CB00008B/1172/J

* 9 7 8 1 4 2 1 8 4 7 5 9 7 *